Children's Occupational Outlook Handbook
Second Edition

CFKR Career Materials
Auburn, CA
(800) 525-5626

Written and Edited By: Linda Schwartz and Toni Wolfgang
Cover Art and Illustrations By: Laurie Barrows
Based on the Department of Labor's Occupational Outlook Handbook

Children's Occupational Outlook Handbook, Second Edition
© Copyright 1999 by CFKR Career Materials, Auburn, CA

For Ordering Information:
CFKR Career Materials
11860 Kemper Road, Unit 7
Auburn, CA 95603
(800) 525-5626

Table of Contents

Mechanics, Installers, and Repairers Occupations Cluster 163

Construction Trades Occupations Cluster 175

Production Occupations Cluster 191

Transportation and Material Moving Occupations 209

Youth Jobs 213

Introduction
To the Teacher

The first edition of the *Children's Occupational Outlook Handbook (COOH)* changed the way educators were able to provide career information to the younger ages. It was a book about what people do for their self-worth, as well as for income to pay their bills. What people choose as their career is a part of a decision-making process which affects the rest of their lives.

This second edition of the COOH has kept the same format as the first edition. The information has been updated. Website addresses have been provided where available.

As with the OOH, the COOH is best used as a reference. Students can start exploring the Table of Contents, looking over the listings for each occupational cluster. The clusters and most job titles follow the OOH, and because jobs are grouped in clusters, it is easy for the student to read about more than one occupation in a general area of interest.

This book was also written to get the minds of our youth thinking about the world around them in an enjoyable way. We have moved into the "information age," in which computers and electronics have an impact on our lives more than we realize. Boys and girls grow into men and women who have more choices than ever before in history. It is a very exciting time to be planning a career; yet in many ways it is more confusing and can be overwhelming.

By starting career awareness at a younger age than when it has historically been introduced, we are helping students start the whole decision-making process earlier. Hopefully, the will make choices which will lead them to satisfying and rewarding careers, through which they will be financially independent and contribute to society.

The following information explains the categories included in each job title:

What They Do - This is a brief and concise description of the job. There are often many more job duties than what are described. Instead of overwhelming the reader, this description gives the reader a good, general idea of what the job entails.

Working Conditions - This category provides more general information of the job, but focuses on the working environment. The most common points of reference in this section are indoors/outdoors; work on evenings/weekends/holidays; stand/sit; and bend/lift/carry.

Education and Training - There are three levels of education and training. See page *viii*, for a legend to describe what each "owl" indicates.

Job Outlook - Three levels are used for the job outlook. Unlike other sources, including the OOH, this rating does more than simply take the expected increase or decrease of employment for the job. As an example, the level of competition must also be considered. These factors have been taken into account to determine the real potential for someone to get a particular job in the first decade of the 21st century. The legend on page *vii* describes what each "hand signal" designates.

Average Earnings - These three levels of earnings are based on the average an individual, with experience, is currently earning. An assumption was made that the general range of future earnings would remain the same as today. For example, if a physician makes high wages today, the same physician will probably earn high wages in 15 years. The three levels used are described on page *vii*.

Related Jobs - Many of the jobs listed in this category are in the COOH or the OOH. Others can be found in the *Dictionary of Occupational Titles,* which will give a description of job duties. This book is available through CFKR Career Materials.

Subjects To Study Now and Later - These general courses will help students evaluate their interests and gain knowledge to get a good start towards that occupation.

Getting Ready and Places to Go to Observe - The ideas presented in this section are to be used as a springboard for further research about jobs. The activities are there not only to teach students something related to the job and also a new awareness about work, family and themselves. Many activities involve doing further research at the library not only because the library is one of the best resources to gain more information, but developing library skills will help the students throughout their lives. Many job titles give the type of business or location where a worker can be found. A student who is able to interview a worker by phone or in person will find suggested questions on page *ix. All activities are to be done with parental or guardian permission and supervision. They are ideas and suggestions only.*

Tell Me More - This category usually provides addresses to write to for more information about the careers. See page *ix* for a sample letter.

Legend for Education and Training, Job Outlook, and Average Earnings

Education and Training

 Up to one year of high school is all that is required to get hired for this job title. There may be jobs for this career which will require additional education.

 Up to approximately four years of education beyond high school and/or training is normally required to get a job in this career.

 It normally takes more than four years of education and/or training to get a job in this career.

Job Outlook

 Excellent -There should be many job openings and a high demand for job seekers for this career. The potential for finding for a job is high.

 Good -There should be job openings for qualified people. Certain geographic areas may provide better opportunities than others. Some of the careers are expected to grow in employment much faster than other jobs, but there may be a lot of competition for the jobs available. On the other hand, some jobs are not expected to grow as fast, but there is such a large turnover, there will be many job openings.

 Low -Either tough competition, little growth, or even a decline in employment is expected for job openings.

Average Earnings

The national average wages for the experienced worker in this job are less than $25,000. Wages will vary between geographic areas.

The national average wages for the experienced worker in this job are between $25,000 and $50,000. Wages will vary between geographic areas.

The national average wages for the experienced worker in this job are more than $50,000. Wages will vary between geographic areas.

Sample Interview Questions and Inquiry Letter

Find out more information by writing to the addresses listed in the "Tell Me More" category. It is important to be as clear as possible when writing for more information about a particular career. It this is a class project, be sure to find out if the information should be sent home or to school. You can use your own words when writing a letter, but here is a sample of one:

January 17, 1999

CFKR Career Materials
11860 Kemper Road, Unit 7
Auburn, CA 95603

To Whom It May Concern:

I am researching careers in my class. I am very interested in learning more about being a Guidance Counselor. If you have any information about this career, including job duties and education, please send it to my attention at the address below.

Thank you very much for your help.

Sincerely,

What A. Student

What A. Student
5555 Your Street
Your Town, ST 12345

If you want to have what's called an information interview on the telephone or in person with someone, call the business and explain that you are studying careers and would like to interview someone in a specific occupation. Below are a few suggested questions when you do the interview. There are many more questions you can ask. Write down your questions before you interview the person. Remember to send a thank you note to the person after the interview.

- What are you job duties?
- What do you like about your job?
- What do you dislike about your job?
- What hours do you work?
- Do you travel?
- How long did you go to school? What subjects did you study?
- Did you get on-the-job training?
- What suggestions do you have for someone like me who is interested in working in this job?

Executive, Administrative, and Managerial Occupations

These jobs often require training, managing, and directing other workers. Other duties include problem solving, handling business records, and planning and directing projects. Most jobs require a minimum of a bachelor's degree. The earnings are usually in the medium to high range.

Accountants

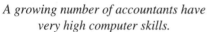

A growing number of accountants have very high computer skills.

  Education and Training:

A four year college degree is usually required. A master's degree or certification is very helpful when looking for a job.

 Job Outlook:

Excellent

  Average Earnings:

Medium

What They Do: Accountants help businesses, the government, and individuals prepare records of how their money is spent. Accountants also prepare records showing how much money is earned and paid in taxes. Accountants work with numbers. They often use computers which help reduce the amount of calculations needed for the records. Many accountants work for a branch of the government.

Working Conditions: Accountants sit most of the time indoors at a desk. Accountants who specialize in taxes work long hours during the tax season.

Related Jobs: Appraiser, budget officer, loan officer, bank officer, actuary, underwriter, and purchasing agent

Subjects To Study Now and Later: Mathematics, computer science, business, and English

Getting Ready and Places to Go to Observe: Ask your parents if you can try to balance their checkbooks. Borrow a book from the library and set up a bookkeeping system with your own money and savings. Ask local business owners how they keep track of their money. Find out if they use an accountant. Banks use accountants often. They like to help their customers and may talk with you about the work accountants do at their company.

 Tell Me More:
Institute of Management
   Accountants
10 Paragon Drive
Montvale, NJ 07645-1760
http://www.imanet.org

American Institute of Certified Public
   Accountants
Harborside Financial Center
201 Plaza III
Jersey City, NJ 07311-3881
http://www.aicpa.org

Administrative Services Managers

Education and Training:

Educational requirements vary from a high school diploma to a bachelor's degree. Work experience is very important.

Job Outlook:

Poor

Average Earnings:

Medium

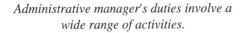

Administrative manager's duties involve a wide range of activities.

What They Do: Administrative services managers coordinate and manage supportive services. This means they may be responsible for secretarial services, mail, conference planning, supplies, printing, food, parking, and other departments. They must make sure duties are performed on schedule and goals are met. In large companies and governments, the supervisors of these individual departments report to the administrative services manager. In small companies, there may be one person in charge of all these areas with no supervisor between the workers and the manager.

Working Conditions: Administrative services managers work indoors in comfortable offices. In large companies, they may travel a lot.

Related Jobs: Appraiser, buyer, clerical supervisor, cost estimator, purchasing manager, and property and real estate manager

Subjects To Study Now and Later: Mathematics, English, economics, computer operations, keyboarding, and business

Getting Ready and Places to Go to Observe: Answering the telephone, bringing in the mail, paying the bills, taking care of the yard and many other things can be considered support services for your home. Have a family meeting to set goals for when chores are to be done. How can schedules and goals be improved? Large businesses are where you will usually find an administrative services manager, but it is the small businesses where you will have a better chance of seeing first hand what they do.

Tell Me More:
International Facility Management Association
1 East Greenway Plaza, Suite 1100
Houston, TX 77046-0194
http://ifma.org

Construction Managers

  Education and Training:

Companies look for industry experience with a bachelor's degree in construction or building science.

 Job Outlook:

Good

 Average Earnings:

Medium - High

Construction managers track costs and budget the time required to meet deadlines.

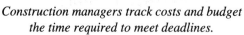

What They Do: Construction managers plan, budget, and direct a construction project. They schedule all the activities that are involved in the construction project. They plan how long each step of the project will take. Construction managers also hire and dismiss as needed the workers and companies who specialize in a part of the construction. Construction managers make sure materials arrive correctly and on time. They are also responsible for making sure all necessary permits have been issued and all building and safety codes are met during construction.

Working Conditions: Construction managers work indoors in an office and outdoors at the construction site. It is a fast-paced environment. They often work more than 40 hours.

Related Jobs: Architect, civil engineer, construction supervisor, cost engineer, developer, electrical engineer, and mechanical engineer

Subjects To Study Now and Later: English, mathematics, drafting, chemistry, physics, different shop classes, and business

Getting Ready and Places to Go to Observe: Construction managers have a great deal of experience in many areas of construction, also known as a craft, such as plumbing or carpentry. If you enjoy a related area, such as working with wood, ask a parent if you can learn more about it. Materials can be found around the home. Visit a construction site with an adult.

Tell Me More:
Associated Builders and Contractors
1300 North 17th St.
Rosslyn, VA 22209
http://www.abc.org

Construction Management
 Association of America
7918 Jones Branch Dr., Suite 540
McLean, VA 22102
http://www.access.digex.net~cmaa

Education Administrators

Education administrators set educational goals and evaluate teachers and other staff.

Education and Training:

Most jobs require a master's degree or doctorate. Work experience is very important.

Job Outlook:

Poor

Average Earnings:

Medium - High

What They Do: Education administrators provide, manage, and lead educational activities in schools, colleges, museums, and in the community. They are principals in the public schools, department heads in colleges, and superintendents in school district offices. They help set educational goals and the procedures to meet them. They also help train and motivate teachers and staff. Other responsibilities such as budgets, relations with parents, and overseeing supervisors of staff, coaches, and librarians often belong to the education administrator.

Working Conditions: Education administrators work indoors in offices. They usually work more than 40 hours a week, including nights and weekends, when school activities take place.

Related Jobs: Health services administrator, social service agency administrator, recreation and park manager, museum director, and library director

Subjects To Study Now and Later: English, history, mathematics, and science

Getting Ready and Places to Go to Observe: A good education is the most important thing you can do now to get ready for this type of career. Participate in class, read, take care in doing your school work and homework assignments. Let the principal of your school know of your interests. Ask your principal and assistant principal about their job, their duties, and the work experience they had before becoming a principal.

Tell Me More:
American Federation of School
  Administrators
1729 21st St. NW
Washington, DC 20009

American Association of School
  Administrators
1801 North Moore St.
Arlington, VA 22209

Work experience is a requirement for becoming an engineering, science, or computer systems manager.

Education and Training:

A bachelor's degree is the minimum required. Many companies require a master's degree or Ph.D. In addition, many years of work experience is also necessary.

Job Outlook:

Excellent

Average Earnings:

High

What They Do: Engineering, science and computer systems managers plan and coordinate various activities. Some of these activities may involve research, development, and computers. These managers help make goals and plans to meet the goals. Engineering managers may supervise people who design machinery. Science managers may oversee activities in agricultural science, chemistry, biology, geology, meteorology or physics. Computer systems managers plan computer-related activities in an organization, including the development of computer hardware and software.

Working Conditions: Engineering, science and computer systems managers usually work in offices or laboratories. Many must work over 40 hours a week to meet deadlines.

Related Jobs: Engineer, natural scientist, computer personnel, mathematician, general manager, and top executive

Subjects To Study Now and Later: English, mathematics, computers, chemistry, physics, biology, and business

Getting Ready and Places to Go to Observe: Read as much as you can about the various sciences and engineering topics that interest you. These topics can include bridges, aeronautics, computers, holograms, genetics and many, many more topics.

Tell Me More:
IEEE Computer Society
Headquarters Office
1730 Massachusetts Ave., NW
Washington, DC 20036-1992

Send a self-addressed business-size envelope with 6 first-class stamps affixed to:
Junior Engineering Technical
Society (JETS-Guidance)
1420 King St., Suite 405
Alexandria, VA 22314-2794
http://www.asee.org/jets

Education and Training:

Farmers may have experience from growing up or working on a farm. Completing a two- or four-year program at a college of agriculture is increasingly important.

Job Outlook:

Poor

Average Earnings:

Low - Medium

Farmers' incomes vary greatly from year to year.

What They Do: Farmers produce food and fiber for our nation and for selling to other countries. Duties of farmers on crop farms include planting, tilling, fertilizing, and harvesting. On farms with animals, farmers feed and take care of the animals, and maintain the pens and barns. On horticultural farms, they take care of growing plants, flowers, fruits and vegetables. Farmers make many managerial decisions. They must carefully plan their crops, which can be influenced by the weather, disease, and other factors.

Working Conditions: Many farmers work long hours during certain seasons. During the seasons which aren't as busy, some operators also have other jobs not on the farm. Farmers with animals work daily year around to care for them.

Related Jobs: Agricultural engineer, animal breeder, dairy scientist, plant breeder and poultry scientist

Subjects To Study Now and Later: English, mathematics, science, biology, botany, agriculture, business and computers

Getting Ready and Places to Go to Observe: Join youth organizations like Future Farmers of America and 4-H Clubs in your area. Take care of an animal or tend a garden to see if you like the work of a farm operator. Visit farms in your area for a tour. Some farms may have working summer camps for kids. Stay for a week and get hands-on experience of working on a farm.

Tell Me More:
American Farm Bureau Federation
225 Touhy Ave.
Park Ridge, IL 60068
http://www.fb.com

American Society of Farm Managers
and Rural Appraisers
950 South Cherry St., Suite 508
Denver, CO 80222
http://www.agriassociations.org

Financial Managers

  Education and Training:

A bachelor's degree is the minimum required. Many companies require a master's degree.

 Job Outlook:

Poor

 Average Earnings:

Medium - High

Financial manager positions usually require substantial experience.

What They Do: Financial managers plan, write reports and take care of the money in a company. In large companies the financial manager is the supervisor of others who help take care of the money. They are the ones that write checks, deposit money, and keep records. In smaller companies one person does all these jobs. Large businesses may have more than one financial manager.

Working Conditions: Financial managers work indoors in offices. In large companies, some travel is needed.

Related Jobs: Accountant, auditor, budget officer, credit analyst, loan officer, insurance consultant, pension consultant, real estate advisor, securities analyst, and underwriter

Subjects To Study Now and Later: English, mathematics, computer science, business, and accounting classes

Getting Ready and Places to Go to Observe: Have fun at home by keeping a chart of the allowance or money you have to spend and save. Open or add to a savings account at a local bank. Set up a plan for at least one month and keep careful notes about saving and spending. Keep track of extra ways you make money at garage sales, recycling, or odd jobs. Visit a local bank and business and ask them if they have more than one financial manager. How are large companies and small companies different in the way they operate?

 Tell Me More:
American Bankers Association
1120 Connecticut Ave. NW
Washington, DC 20036

Financial Management Association, International
College of Business Administration
University of South Florida
Tampa, FL 33620-5500

General Managers

Education and Training:

A bachelor's degree is required for this occupation.

Job Outlook:

Good, with competition for top managerial jobs.

Average Earnings:

Medium - High

General managers oversee and strive to motivate workers.

What They Do: General managers are in charge of making the rules and setting the goals that help run their company. They go to meetings and watch over the work of others in the company. They may have additional responsibilities in small companies, such as buying supplies, hiring and training people and keeping track of inventory.

Working Conditions: General managers usually work inside an office at a desk. Some work evenings and weekends. Lots of travel is needed for general managers in large companies that have many locations.

Related Jobs: Postmaster, chief executive officer, hotel manager, and financial manager

Subjects To Study Now and Later: English, mathematics, computer science, and business classes

Getting Ready and Places to Go to Observe: Being a class officer or representative at your school will give you experience in leading others. Helping to organize a class project or fundraiser gives you experience in working with others. Local businesses, supermarkets, and the post office have general managers that are in charge.

Tell Me More:

American Management Association
Management Information Service
1601 Broadway
New York, NY 10019-7420

National Management Association
2210 Arbor Blvd.
Dayton, OH 45439

Hotel Managers

Many hotel managers work considerably more than 40 hours per week.

  Education and Training:

Most need a two- or four-year degree in a hotel management program.

 Job Outlook:

Excellent

 Average Earnings:

Medium - High

What They Do: Hotel managers are responsible for making sure hotels and motels are running correctly and making a profit. A hotel guest's visit should be pleasant. The rooms must be clean. Pools, tennis courts, ice machines, and anything else at the hotel that is for the convenience and pleasure of the guest should be in good working order. Managers are also responsible for hiring workers and supervising them. In small hotels or motels, the manager may be involved in everything related to the hotel or motel. In large hotels, there are assistants that help run the hotel.

Working Conditions: Hotel managers often work nights and weekends. A few people become hotel managers through work experience.

Related Jobs: Restaurant manager, apartment building manager, department store manager, and office manager

Subjects To Study Now and Later: English, mathematics, business, foreign languages, psychology, and speech

Getting Ready and Places to Go to Observe: Hotel managers are concerned with organizing a business that serves people. How can the organization in your home be changed in a way that will increase the pleasure of each member in your family? Talk to your parents about experimenting with this idea. If you ever stay in motels or hotels when on vacation with your family, you can observe some of the duties of the employees. Ask questions about how they spend their workday. What is their educational background and work experience?

 Tell Me More:

Council on Hotel, Restaurant, and
   Institutional Education
1200 17th St. NW
Washington, DC 20036-3097

The American Hotel and Motel
   Association (AH&MA)
Information Center
1201 New York Ave., NW
Washington, DC 20005-3931

Education and Training:

A bachelor's degree is preferred. Some companies will train people with a high school diploma.

Job Outlook:

Poor

Average Earnings:

Medium

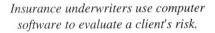

Insurance underwriters use computer software to evaluate a client's risk.

What They Do: Insurance underwriters work for insurance companies. They review information on applications from people who want to insure property or people. The information reviewed inform the underwriter if a person is very likely to make a claim. If an insurance underwriter approves too many people who make claims, the insurance company may lose money. If they approve a lot of people who do not make claims, then the company makes money.

Working Conditions: Insurance underwriters work indoors in comfortable offices. They sit a lot. Some travel to inspect work areas to help them decide whether or not to approve the application for insurance coverage.

Related Jobs: Auditor, budget analyst, financial advisor, loan officer, credit manager, real estate appraiser, and risk manager

Subjects To Study Now and Later: Mathematics, business, English, computer science, and psychology

Getting Ready and Places to Go to Observe: If you want to insure your home, an underwriter would decide whether or not to insure it. They consider if there are working smoke alarms, deadbolt locks on the doors, and if the home is in good condition. Go over these things in your home and see if you can find other things that make your home a good insurance risk. Call and visit a local insurance sales representative, also known as an insurance agent. Insurance agents work very closely with underwriters and can usually tell you a great deal about the work.

Tell Me More:

American Institute for Chartered Property and Casualty
     Underwriters, and the Insurance Institute of America
720 Providence Rd.
Malvern, PA 19355-0716

Management Analysts

Management analysts advise managers on many types of issues.

 Education and Training:

A master's degree in business education and at least five years experience are usually needed for this job.

 Job Outlook:

Excellent

 Average Earnings:

Medium - High

What They Do: Management analysts and consultants help companies make important decisions and solve problems. They find out information about the company by looking at reports, talking to workers and watching the company operate smoothly. They write reports that give other ideas to help the company run better. Some consultants work in groups; others work alone.

Working Conditions: Management consultants work inside an office at a desk. Travel is often needed.

Related Jobs: Computer systems analyst, operations research analyst, economist, and financial analyst

Subjects To Study Now and Later: English, mathematics, computer science, and business classes

Getting Ready and Places to Go to Observe: Solve a problem at school or home by finding new ways to make it work better or faster or cost less money. Ask your parents or teacher to try this new idea for a day and see if it works. Check with local businesses to find out if they have hired a consultant to help them with their company. Find out what the consultant did to help their company run better.

 Tell Me More:
The Association of Management Consulting Firms
521 Fifth Ave., 35th Floor
New York, NY 10175-3598

Marketing, Advertising, and Public Relations Managers

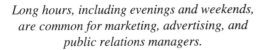
Long hours, including evenings and weekends, are common for marketing, advertising, and public relations managers.

Education and Training:
A bachelor's or master's degree is usually required. Companies usually promote experienced staff to these managerial positions.

Job Outlook:
Good

Average Earnings:
Medium

What They Do: Marketing, advertising and public relations managers oversee the promotion of a product or company. The goal is to either increase sales, increase the public's awareness or to influence the public's opinion. Marketing managers coordinate between the sales and product development manager to monitor trends and develop marketing plans. Advertising managers oversee the development of advertising, such as radio and television commercials and newspaper ads. Public relations managers supervise the public relations specialists within the department.

Working Conditions: Marketing, advertising and public relations managers work long hours in comfortable offices. Travel is often necessary.

Related Jobs: Art director, commercial and graphic artist, copy chief, copywriter, editor, lobbyist, marketing research analyst, public relations specialist, promotion specialist, sales representative and technical writer

Subjects To Study Now and Later: Marketing, psychology, speech, English, computer operations, political science, mathematics

Getting Ready and Places to Go to Observe: Observe the ads you see from a different view. What does a marketing manager want you to think as you watch television commercials or read ads in a magazine? Pick a favorite large corporation (for example, fast food restaurants or sports equipment companies) and follow their advertising campaigns. Look for articles about this company in the newspaper or magazines. Look at these from the company's viewpoint.

Tell Me More:

American Marketing Association
250 S. Wacker Dr.
Chicago, IL 60606

American Advertising Federation
Education Services Department
1101 Vermont Ave. NW, Suite 500
Washington, DC 20005

Property Managers

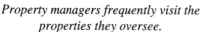

Property managers frequently visit the properties they oversee.

Education and Training:

College degrees are preferred. On-site managers begin at a smaller property or as an assistant manager at a large property.

Job Outlook:

Excellent

Average Earnings:

High

What They Do: Property managers handle the day-to-day duties of managing property, such as apartment and office buildings, which brings in an income from renters or leasers. Property managers usually manage more than one property at a time. They advertise for tenants and work out their rental or lease agreements. They also collect rent payments, take care of the bookkeeping for the property and make sure all maintenance bills are paid on time. All services for the property, such as security and trash removal, are also handled by the property manager.

Working Conditions: Property managers work indoors in comfortable offices. They spend a lot of time visiting the property they manage.

Related Jobs: Restaurant and food service manager, hotel and resort manager, health services manager, education administrator, and city manager

Subjects To Study Now and Later: Mathematics, computer science, English, and business courses

Getting Ready and Places to Go to Observe: Help take care of the property at your home. Yard work, repairs, and cleaning are always needed. Taking care of property is a lot of responsibility and work. Visit a large and a small apartment building in your area. Ask if you can talk to the manager. Find out if they have a property manager and if the manager lives in the building. What are the differences between the two?

Tell Me More:

Building Owners and Managers Institute International
1521 Ritchie Hwy.
Arnold, MD 21012
http://www.bomi-edu.org

Restaurant Managers

Restaurant managers check the quality and quantity of refrigerated foods.

Education and Training:

Work experience is very important. Many start as trainees after completing a two- or four-year educational program.

Job Outlook:

Excellent

Average Earnings:

Medium

What They Do: Restaurant managers are responsible for making sure a restaurant operates smoothly and makes money. They hire and train the workers. They make sure food is ordered, kept fresh, and prepared properly. Restaurant managers resolve complaints from customers. Many of the purchases, including food and equipment, is also taken care of by the manager. They may also prepare bank deposits, and other bookkeeping and record keeping duties. When the restaurant is busy, the manager may help wash dishes, clean tables, cook, or help wherever it is needed.

Working Conditions: Restaurant managers work indoors in restaurants. They may work evenings, weekends, and holidays. Their workdays are often long and they sometimes work more than 40 hours a week.

Related Jobs: Hotel manager, health services administrator, retail store manager, and bank manager

Subjects To Study Now and Later: Business, English, foreign languages, psychology, public speaking, and social studies

Getting Ready and Places to Go to Observe: Ask if you can manage the kitchen in your home for one day. You will need to plan the meals for that day. Make sure all the needed food is available. Prepare and serve the meals. Clean up the table and kitchen after each meal. Be very observant whenever you go to a restaurant. How do the waitpersons talk to you? Watch all the workers and notice what kind of job duties there are in a restaurant. Can you tell which person is the manager?

Tell Me More:

The Educational Foundation of the
    National Restaurant Association
250 South Wacker Dr., Suite 1400
Chicago, IL 60606

Council on Hotel, Restaurant and
    Institutional Education
1200 17th St. NW
Washington, DC 20036-3097

Professional Specialty Occupations

This is the largest cluster of workers in the book. Workers in these occupations perform a wide variety of duties. They work in almost every type of business. Job openings for these occupations will probably increase much more than many other types of occupations. The workers in this cluster usually have a lot of responsibility.

Aircraft Pilots

 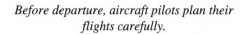

Education and Training:

Most airline companies prefer to hire college graduates. They require 1,500 hours of flying experience and passing various tests. A commercial pilot's license to fly cargo or people requires 250 hours of flying.

Job Outlook:

Poor

Before departure, aircraft pilots plan their flights carefully.

Average Earnings:

High

What They Do: Aircraft pilots fly airplanes and helicopters. They move people, cargo, and mail. Helicopter pilots fight fires and help with police and rescue work. On large aircraft there are usually two pilots in the cockpit. The captain is in charge and the copilot helps with the instruments, flying the plane, and talking to the air traffic controllers. Sometimes a third pilot, the flight engineer, helps with repairs and watching for other aircraft. Pilots plan their flights and check the weather. They check the engines, controls and cargo. They keep careful records.

Working Conditions: Pilots can not fly over 100 hours per month or more than 1,000 hours per year. They often stay overnight away from home. Pilots fly at all hours of the day and night so working times often change.

Related Jobs: Air traffic controller, dispatcher and navigator

Subjects To Study Now and Later: Mathematics, physics, computer operations, English and foreign languages

Getting Ready and Places to Go to Observe: Do you know someone that has a remote control airplane? Watch them prepare the airplane for flying. Make a list of things that need to be done before the plane can fly. Does it matter if the weather is rainy or windy? Visit an airport or military base to see pilots coming and going. If you are taking a trip by airplane have an adult ask if you can go into the cockpit and talk to the pilots. How can you tell who is the captain and who is the copilot?

Tell Me More:

Airline Pilots Association
1625 Massachusetts Ave. NW
Washington, DC 20036

Helicopter Association
  International
1619 Duke St.
Alexandria, VA 22314

Air Traffic Controllers

Education and Training:

Four years of college or work experience, passing a test, and a 13-week training program are necessary.

Job Outlook:

Poor

Air traffic controllers carefully monitor the movement of each plane.

Average Earnings:

Medium

What They Do: Air traffic controllers keep track of lanes in a certain area. They use radar to make sure all of the planes in the air are a safe space apart. They are in charge of getting all the planes in and out of the airport in a safe and orderly way. Several controllers work together at each control center. Air traffic controllers watch many planes at once and guide them safely. They tell pilots about changes in the weather and other safety information. They also help search for missing aircraft.

Working Conditions: Control centers are open 24 hours per day, seven days a week, so air traffic controllers sometimes work weekends, evenings and holidays. It is sometimes a very stressful job.

Related Jobs: Airline-radio operator, airline dispatcher and navigator

Subjects To Study Now and Later: Mathematics, electronics, physics, computer operations, English and foreign languages

Getting Ready and Places to Go to Observe: Use the library to learn more about how airplanes fly. When you go to the airport look for the air traffic control tower. Can you see the people working inside? Outside look for the ground controller guiding the planes to the terminal and out onto the runway.

Tell Me More:

Contact the Office of personnel Management (OPM) Job Information Center in your area. For a local number, call (912) 757-3000. Ask for a copy of the Traffic Controller Announcement. Or, contact OPM through the internet at *http://www.usajobs.opm.gov*

Aerospace Engineers

Aerospace engineers design, build, and test components for aircraft and spacecraft.

  Education and Training:

A bachelor's degree is needed for this job.

 Job Outlook:

Poor

 Average Earnings:

Medium

What They Do: Aerospace engineers plan, design, test and help make aircraft, missiles, and spacecraft. Sometimes they work on only one type of aircraft like helicopters, spacecraft or rockets. They develop new ideas in aviation, defense systems, and space exploration. Engineers often use computers in their work.

Working Conditions: Aerospace engineers work in laboratories, factories, or testing sites. Some engineers travel to other plants or locations.

Related Jobs: Engineering, science and computer systems managers; physical, life, and computer scientists; mathematicians; engineering and science technicians; and architects

Subjects To Study Now and Later: Mathematics, physics, chemistry, biology, computer science, drafting, industrial arts, and English

Getting Ready and Places to Go to Observe: Check out books from the library and find out how aircrafts are built. Do you know how a plane can fly? You can learn this from books, too. Visit an air force base or space center. California, Washington and Texas have large aerospace manufacturers that sometimes provide tours if you live or visit in those areas. Local museums or exhibit halls may have information on aerospace.

 Tell Me More:

American Institute of Aeronautics
  and Astronautics, Inc.
Suite 500, 1801 Alexander Bell Dr.
Reston, VA 20191-4344

Send a self-addressed business-size envelope with 6 first-class stamps affixed to:
Junior Engineering Technical
Society (JETS-Guidance)
1420 King St., Suite 405
Alexandria, VA 22314-2794
http://www.asee.org/jets

Chemical Engineers

Education and Training:

A bachelor's degree is needed for this job.

Job Outlook:

Good

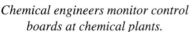

Chemical engineers monitor control boards at chemical plants.

Average Earnings:

Medium

What They Do: Chemical engineers use mathematics, chemistry, and physics to solve problems. They design equipment and find ways to make chemicals. They work in factories to test the way these chemicals are made and oversee the process. Chemical engineers can also work in electronics or aircraft manufacturing. Some work trying to find ways to control pollution.

Working Conditions: Chemical engineers work in laboratories, factories, or testing sites. Some chemical engineers travel to factories or sites.

Related Jobs: Engineering, science and computer systems managers; physical, life, and computer scientists; mathematicians; engineering and science technicians; and architects

Subjects To Study Now and Later: Mathematics, physics, chemistry, biology, computer science, drafting, industrial arts, and English

Getting Ready and Places to Go to Observe: Check out library books to find fun, safe, and easy to do experiments for children. Always have permission from an adult and follow directions carefully. Places to visit are an air force base or space center.

Tell Me More:

American Institute of Chemical
  Engineers
345 East 47th St.
New York, NY 10017-2395

American Chemical Society,
  Career Services
1155 16th St. NW
Washington, DC 20036

Computer Engineers

Computer engineers may work with hardware or software.

  Education and Training:

A bachelor's degree is usually needed. A Ph.D., or a master's degree is required in research laboratories or academic institutions.

 Job Outlook:

Excellent

 Average Earnings:

Medium

What They Do: Computer engineers use science and mathematics to design and build computer parts, software and other computer related systems. They often work as part of a team. Some specialize in hardware, which can range from computer chips to modems. Others specialize in software. Computer engineers may also analyze and solve programming problems.

Working Conditions: Computer engineers usually work in comfortable offices or laboratories. Some are able to work from home.

Related Jobs: Computer programmer, financial analyst, computer systems analyst, urban planner, engineer, mathematician, statistician, operations research analyst, management analyst, and actuary

Subjects To Study Now and Later: Mathematics, chemistry, physics, computer science, and English

Getting Ready and Places to Go to Observe: Read computer magazines to start understanding how a computer works. Go to the library to read more about computers. Many communities offer a variety of computer classes for people of all ages. Check into taking one.

 Tell Me More:
IEEE Computer Society
Headquarters Office
1730 Massachusetts Ave., NW
Washington, DC 20036-1992

Institute for Certification of
Computing Professionals (ICCP)
2200 East Devon Ave., Suite 268
Des Plaines, IL 60018
http://www.iccp.org

Education and Training:

A bachelor's degree is needed for this job.

Job Outlook:

Good

Average Earnings:

Medium - High

Civil engineers work in the oldest branch of engineering.

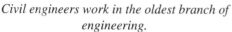

What They Do: Civil engineers plan, design and oversee the building of roads, airports, tunnels, bridges, water and sewage systems, and buildings. They figure out the best way to do the job to save money and check for safety. Some civil engineers are managers, teachers, or researchers.

Working Conditions: Civil engineers often work at construction sites. Some work in distant areas or other countries. In this job you often move from place to place.

Related Jobs: Engineering, science and computer systems managers; physical, life, and computer scientists; mathematicians; engineering and science technicians; and architects

Subjects To Study Now and Later: Mathematics, chemistry, physics, biology, computer science, drafting, industrial arts, and English.

Getting Ready and Places to Go to Observe: Use nearby sand or dirt piles, wood scraps, and building blocks to make small buildings, tunnels and roads. Use a computer to draw your idea. Try different ideas and see which one works the best. Do you know why? Watch new buildings as they are being built in your area. How do they change from one week to the next? Ask if you can talk to the civil engineer for the project.

Tell Me More:

American Society of Civil Engineers
1801 Alexander Bell Dr.
Reston, VA 20191-4400

Electrical Engineers

Electrical engineers design circuits.

 Education and Training:

A bachelor's degree is needed for this job.

 Job Outlook:

Good

 Average Earnings:

Medium

What They Do: Electrical engineers design, develop, test, and oversee the making of electrical equipment. This equipment is used for electric utilities, electric motors, lights, and wiring for buildings, cars and aircraft. They also solve problems and figure out how much time and money projects will cost.

Working Conditions: Electrical engineers work 40 hours per week at manufacturing plants. Overtime is sometimes required to finish a job.

Related Jobs: Engineering, science and computer systems managers; physical, life, and computer scientists; mathematicians; engineering and science technicians; and architects

Subjects To Study Now and Later: Mathematics, chemistry, biology, physics, computer science, drafting, industrial arts, and English

Getting Ready and Places to Go to Observe: Use books from the library to study more about electricity and electronics. Ask your telephone or utility company for a tour. Go to local electronic shops for ideas and simple ways you can make use of electricity.

 Tell Me More:

Institute of Electrical and
    Electronics Engineers
1828 L St., NW, Suite 1202
Washington, DC 20036

Send a self-addressed business-size envelope with 6 first-class stamps affixed to:
Junior Engineering Technical
Society (JETS-Guidance)
1420 King St., Suite 405
Alexandria, VA 22314-2794
http://www.asee.org/jets

Engineering Technicians

Engineering technicians solve problems using scientific and engineering principles.

Education and Training:

Most engineering technicians get training from technical schools or colleges. This usually takes two years. Some people learn the job while working. Others take special classes by mail.

 Job Outlook:

Good

 Average Earnings:

Medium

What They Do:　Engineering technicians use rules of science, engineering and math to solve problems. They work in manufacturing, sales, design, and service. Some engineering technicians help engineers and scientists do research and experiments. They also may work in the areas of civil, electronics, industrial, and mechanical engineering. Engineering technicians also design and run tests to check the quality of products.

Working Conditions:　Engineering technicians work 40 hours per week. They work indoors in laboratories, offices, electronics shops, plants and outdoors at construction sites. Some technicians travel to other companies to work.

Related Jobs:　Science technician, drafter, surveyor, and broadcast technician

Subjects To Study Now and Later:　Mathematics, science, physics, computer operations, electronics, and English

Getting Ready and Places to Go to Observe:　Get books at the library that have easy to do projects that you can build. Visit a local electronics store for more ideas. Pick a project, put it together and test it. If it doesn't work quite right, find out why by asking questions and trying other ways to make it work better or faster. There are engineering technicians in many different places. Factories where radios, televisions, or computers are made use an engineering technician.

Tell Me More:

Accreditation Board for
　Engineering and Technology
111 Market Place, Suite 1050
Baltimore, MD 21202

Send a self-addressed business-size envelope with 6 first-class stamps affixed to:
Junior Engineering Technical
　Society (JETS-Guidance)
1420 King St., Suite 405
Alexandria, VA 22314-2794
http://www.asee.org/jets

Industrial Engineers

Industrial engineers find ways to make the company run better.

  Education and Training:

A bachelor's degree is needed for this occupation.

 Job Outlook:

Good

 Average Earnings:

Medium

What They Do: Industrial engineers find better ways for companies to make use of workers, machines, material, knowledge and energy. They work more with people than other engineers who work more with products. They design computer programs that help companies make better products in less time and save money. Manufacturing companies, banks, and hospitals often hire industrial engineers to solve problems.

Working Conditions: Industrial engineers work in offices. They sometimes work evenings and weekends.

Related Jobs: Engineering, science and computer systems managers; physical, life, and computer scientists; mathematicians; engineering and science technicians; and architects

Subjects To Study Now and Later: Mathematics, English, biology, chemistry, drafting, computer science, and physics

Getting Ready and Places to Go to Observe: Problem solving at school and home gives you experience in finding new ways to solve problems. Learning about computers and studying mathematics will also be helpful. If you live near a university, find out if they offer degrees in industrial engineering.

 Tell Me More:

Institute of Industrial Engineers, Inc.
25 Technology Park/Atlanta
Norcross, GA 30092
http://www.iienet.org

Send a self-addressed business-size envelope with 6 first-class stamps affixed to:
Junior Engineering Technical
  Society (JETS-Guidance)
1420 King St., Suite 405
Alexandria, VA 22314-2794
http://www.asee.org/jets

Education and Training:

A bachelor's degree and often more education and training are required.

Job Outlook:

Good

Average Earnings:

Medium

Materials engineers search for flaws in newly designed materials.

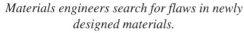

What They Do: Materials engineers review materials to make new and useful products. These engineers also plan new methods to make materials. They test materials for strength or weight. Materials planned or reviewed may be used on products such as aircraft and golf clubs.

Working Conditions: Materials engineers work in laboratories and offices. Some work outdoors part of the time.

Related Jobs: Engineering, science and computer systems managers; physical, life, and computer scientists; mathematicians; engineering and science technicians; and architects

Subjects To Study Now and Later: Mathematics, English, biology, physics, chemistry, and drafting

Getting Ready and Places to Go to Observe: Materials engineers learn how to make products using various materials. Use paper to make something, like an envelope, paper cup, or other useful item. Find out if there is an engineering school or college that you can visit to learn more about engineering.

Tell Me More:

The Minerals, Metals, &
    Materials Foundation
420 Commonwealth Dr.
Warrendale, PA 15086-7514

ASM International
Student Outreach Program
Materials Park, OH 44073-0002

Mechanical Engineers

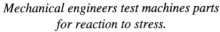

*Mechanical engineers test machines parts
for reaction to stress.*

 Education and Training:

A bachelor's degree is needed for this job.

 Job Outlook:

Good

 Average Earnings:

Medium

What They Do: Mechanical engineers work with creating and transmitting mechanical power and heat. They design and make power-producing machines, like jet and rocket engines. They develop robots, machines that use refrigeration and air-conditioning equipment, and industrial producing equipment.

Working Conditions: Mechanical engineers work indoors, usually in manufacturing plants.

Related Jobs: Engineering, science and computer systems managers; physical, life, and computer scientists; mathematicians; engineering and science technicians; and architects

Subjects To Study Now and Later: Mathematics, computer science, biology, chemistry, physics, drafting, and English

Getting Ready and Places to Go to Observe: Books from the library can help you learn about all types of engineers and the different jobs they do. Find out if there is an engineering school or college in your area that can give you more information about this career.

 Tell Me More:

The American Society of Mechanical Engineers
345 E. 47th St.
New York, NY 10017

American Society of Heating, Refrigeration, and Air-Conditioning Engineers, Inc.
1791 Tullie Circle, NE
Atlanta, GA 30329
http://www.achrae.org

Mining engineers examine the quality of coal deposits.

Education and Training:

A bachelor's degree and often more education and training are required.

Job Outlook:

Good

Average Earnings:

Medium

What They Do: Mining engineers find, remove and prepare minerals for manufacturing companies. They plan and are in charge of constructing mines, tunnels and open pits. Mining engineers must be sure mines are safe for the workers, safe for the earth and affordable for businesses.

Working Conditions: Mining engineers work in laboratories, offices, and outdoors. 40-hour work weeks are normal, but sometimes longer hours are necessary.

Related Jobs: Engineering, science and computer systems managers; physical, life, and computer scientists; mathematicians; engineering and science technicians; and architects

Subjects To Study Now and Later: Mathematics, English, biology, geology, physics, chemistry, and drafting

Getting Ready and Places to Go to Observe: Start a rock collection. Learning about the earth is important to mining engineers. Learn how rocks were formed.

Tell Me More:

The Society for Mining, Metallurgy, and Exploration, Inc.
P.O. Box 625002
Littleton, CO 80162-5002

Send a self-addressed business-size envelope with 6 first-class stamps affixed to:
Junior Engineering Technical Society (JETS-Guidance)
1420 King St., Suite 405
Alexandria, VA 22314-2794
http://www.asee.org/jets

Nuclear Engineers

Nuclear engineers research nuclear energy and radiation.

Education and Training:

A bachelor's degree and often more education and training are required.

Job Outlook:

Good, even though employment will have limited growth.

Average Earnings:

Medium

What They Do: Nuclear engineers study nuclear energy and radiation. They plan and operate nuclear power plants. These plants provide electricity. Some engineers plan nuclear weapons. Others find medical uses for materials and machinery which use radiation.

Working Conditions: Many engineers work in laboratories. Some work in an office all of the time. Others work outdoors part of the time. 40-hour work weeks are normal, but sometimes longer hours and high stress are part of the job.

Related Jobs: Engineering, science and computer systems managers; physical, life, and computer scientists; mathematicians; engineering and science technicians; and architects

Subjects To Study Now and Later: Mathematics, English, biology, physics, chemistry, and drafting

Getting Ready and Places to Go to Observe: Being creative is a part of the engineer's job. Safe home science kits will encourage learning. Borrow books for ideas on how to bring science into your home. Read and write a lot, since these skills are also important.

Tell Me More:

American Nuclear Society
555 North Kensington Ave.
LaGrange Park, IL 60525

Send a self-addressed business-size envelope with 6 first-class stamps affixed to:
Junior Engineering Technical
    Society (JETS-Guidance)
1420 King St., Suite 405
Alexandria, VA 22314-2794
http://www.asee.org/jets

Petroleum engineers interpret seismic recordings in the search for oil.

Education and Training:

A bachelor's degree and often more education and training are required.

Job Outlook:

Good

Average Earnings:

Medium

What They Do: Petroleum engineers look for and produce oil and natural gas. They find the best way to get oil or gas from the earth. Petroleum engineers may be hired by the government, oil companies or consulting firms. Most work where oil and gas are found. This includes Texas, Oklahoma, Louisiana, California, offshore sites, and other countries.

Working Conditions: Many engineers work in laboratories. Some work in an office all of the time. Others work outdoors part of the time. 40-hour work weeks are normal, but sometimes longer hours and high stress are part of the job.

Related Jobs: Engineering, science and computer systems managers; physical, life, and computer scientists; mathematicians; engineering and science technicians; and architects

Subjects To Study Now and Later: Mathematics, English, biology, geology, physics, chemistry, and drafting

Getting Ready and Places to Go to Observe: Oil is used to make many products, and the search for oil is an interesting topic. Talk to the librarians at your public and school libraries about your interest in this field. There should be books with good information available.

Tell Me More:

Society of Petroleum Engineers
222 Palisades Creek Dr.
Richardson, TX 75080-3836

Send a self-addressed business-size envelope with 6 first-class stamps affixed to:
Junior Engineering Technical
Society (JETS-Guidance)
1420 King St., Suite 405
Alexandria, VA 22314-2794
http://www.asee.org/jets

Architects

An architect designs buildings.

 Education and Training:
The majority of all architecture degrees are from 5-year Bachelor of Architecture programs.

 Job Outlook:
Good

 Average Earnings:
Medium - High

What They Do: Architects plan the making of a building. They must know if it is safe, affordable, and meets the needs of those who will be using the building. It may be a house, office or any other building. An architect first learns the needs of the people paying for the building. Then, the architect prepares drawings and final paperwork with all the details of the building.

Working Conditions: Architects spend most of their time in comfortable offices. They meet with clients and other architects. Sometimes they work outdoors at construction sites.

Related Jobs: Landscape architect, building contractor, civil engineer, urban planner, interior and industrial designer, and graphic design

Subjects To Study Now and Later: Mathematics, biology, art, drafting, and English

Getting Ready and Places to Go to Observe: Make small buildings using clay, mud, wood, sticks, or anything else you can find. Make your house with as much detail as you can. Go to your library to find history books on architecture. The planning department of your city might let you look at final drawings and papers for buildings in your city. Visit historical buildings to see their special features. Think about how useful these buildings were when they were built.

Tell Me More:
Society of American Registered
   Architects
Nathan Kolodny Consultants
100 Pinewood Rd., Suite 2A
Hartsdale, NY 10530

Careers in Architecture Program
The American Institute of Architects
1735 New York Ave. NW
Washington, DC 20006
http://www.aiaonline.com

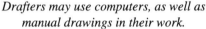

Drafters may use computers, as well as manual drawings in their work.

  Education and Training:

Drafters need to attend two to four years of college after high school. They also get more training on-the-job.

 Job Outlook:

Poor

 Average Earnings:

Medium

What They Do: Drafters prepare detailed drawings used by workers to build bridges, buildings, houses, and spacecraft. Their drawings are also used to manufacture products and machinery. Drafters use information from engineers, architects and scientists to draw the details needed in building or putting together the parts in a machine. Tools they use may be a computer drafting board, compass, and triangle. Drafters usually work in a specific field, such as electrical and mechanical.

Working Conditions: Drafters work indoors in comfortable rooms. They usually sit for long times at a drafting board or computer.

Related Jobs: Architect, landscape architect, engineer, engineering technician, science technician, and surveyor

Subjects To Study Now and Later: Mathematics, English, biology, design, drafting, computer science, and industrial arts

Getting Ready and Places to Go to Observe: Using a paper and pencil try drawing a building or simple machine that shows all the parts needed to put it together. Be neat and very exact about your drawing so others can tell how to make the building or machine from your plans. If possible try using a computer to draw the same plan. There may be several types of drafters at work in your area. Look for new schools, building, roads or bridges being built. Watch for a sign showing what company is doing the work. Call them and ask who did the drafting for the project.

 Tell Me More:

Accrediting Commission of Career Schools and Colleges of Technology
2101 Wilson Blvd., Suite 302
Arlington, VA 22201

Landscape Architects

Landscape architects spend most of their time in offices creating plans and designs.

 Education and Training:

A bachelor's degree and often a master's degree is necessary. Many employers prefer to hire landscape architects who have completed at least one internship.

 Job Outlook:

Good

 Average Earnings:

Medium

What They Do: Landscape architects work with architects and engineers to help determine the best arrangement of roads and buildings. Then, landscape architects design the plans for the plants, walkways, outdoor lights, drainage, and anything that affects the outside of the structure. They must understand the natural surroundings of the location of the structure. This includes soil, animals, trees, plants, and slope of the land. It is also important to know the needs of the client and understand how the structure and surrounding land is going to be used.

Working Conditions: Landscape architects spend a lot of their time indoors in offices and some time outdoors visiting project sites. Some may need to travel to project sites.

Related Jobs: Architect, surveyor, soil conservationist, civil engineer, urban and regional planner, botanist, and horticulturist

Subjects To Study Now and Later: Geology, mathematics, English, biology, botany, design, graphics, mechanical drawing, art, and speech

Getting Ready and Places to Go to Observe: An appreciation for nature is important for this career. Find out if there are areas to take nature walks near where you live. There are books at the library which can help you identify the plants and trees in your area. Watch for the landscaping to begin when you see new construction near where you live. Try to go at different times to watch. How would you have landscaped it differently? Why do you think the landscape architect put walkways and plants in the places you see them?

 Tell Me More:
American Society of Landscape
  Architects
4401 Connecticut Ave. NW
Suite 500
Washington, DC 20008

Council of Landscape Architectural
  Registration Boards
12700 Fair Lakes Circle, Suite 110
Fairfax, VA 22033
Email: *clarb2@aol.com*

Surveyors

Surveyors make sure that a new roadway is on course.

Education and Training:

A one- to three-year program in a junior college or vocational school is the minimum requirement. A 4-year degree is becoming a prerequisite.

Job Outlook:

Good, but employment is expected to slightly decline.

Average Earnings:

Low - Medium

What They Do: Surveyors measure the earth's surface. They determine land, air space and water boundaries. Some surveyors are technicians who use surveying tools to collect information which helps determine boundaries. They measure the height of mountains. Surveyors write descriptions of lands for legal papers and measure construction and mineral sites. Surveyors are using a new satellite system called Global Positioning System (GPS) to help them in their work. GPS uses radio signals transmitted by satellites to precisely locate points on the earth.

Working Conditions: Surveyors work indoors and outdoors. They may walk long distances and stand for long periods. Work is done in all types of weather. When working indoors, surveyors work with computers.

Related Jobs: Civil engineer, architect, mapping scientist, geologist, and geographer

Subjects To Study Now and Later: Mathematics, geography, drafting, mechanical drawing, computer science, and English

Getting Ready and Places to Go to Observe: Have a map with you while travelling in the car, especially on vacation. Also, get a topographical map of the area you live in and the area where you will be vacationing. Use the maps to follow your location as you drive. Topographical maps will indicate the different elevations, too. Contact your city government to find out when surveyors may be in your area. Also, many stores carry personal GPS receivers. Find out if you know anyone who has one and can show you how they work.

Tell Me More:

American Congress on Surveying and Mapping
5410 Grosvenor Lane
Bethesda, MD 20814-2122

Actuaries

 Education and Training:

A bachelor's degree and passing several exams are necessary for this career.

 Job Outlook:

Good

Strong problem-solving skills are important for actuaries.

 Average Earnings:

Medium

What They Do: Actuaries collect and study information. They try to learn what the chances are that people will get ill, have an accident, or have damage to property. Using this information, they help write insurance and retirement plans. Actuaries work for insurance companies, hospitals, and government agencies.

Working Conditions: Actuaries work indoors at a desk. They often use computers. This job may require travelling to meet clients.

Related Jobs: Accountant, economist, financial analyst, mathematician, and statistician

Subjects To Study Now and Later: Mathematics, physics, chemistry, biology, computer sciences, and English

Getting Ready and Places to Go to Observe: If you like working with mathematics and computers you have some interests that actuaries have. Play games that involve mathematics. Use a computer whenever you can. Actuaries often work for large insurance companies, businesses, or government agencies. Ask a local insurance agent for information on this career.

 Tell Me More:

American Academy of Actuaries
1100 17th St. NW, 7th Floor
Washington, DC 20036

Society of Actuaries
475 N. Martingale Rd., Suite 800
Schaumburg, IL 60173-2226

Computer Programmers

  Education and Training:

A bachelor's degree and work experience are usually required.

 Job Outlook:

Excellent

Computer programmers test programs to make sure that the instructions are correct.

 Average Earnings:

Medium

What They Do: Computer programmers write, update and keep care of the directions that list the way the computer runs. They write and test new programs for the computer to follow. If they find mistakes they go back and rewrite the program and test it again. Some programs can be written in a few hours and others may take a year to write.

Working Conditions: Programmers work indoors in comfortable offices. They sometimes work early in the morning or late in the evening to get a project done.

Related Jobs: Statistician, computer engineer, financial analyst, accountant, auditor, actuary, and operations research analyst

Subjects To Study Now and Later: Mathematics, physics, chemistry, biology, computer science, electronics, English, and foreign languages

Getting Ready and Places to Go to Observe: Use a computer as much as you can to play games, do homework, and write letters. Read the manuals and find out all you can about how the computer works. Ask lots of questions and find out just how easy using a computer can be. Many local businesses in your area have used a computer programmer at one time or another for their computer problems. The next time you are in a business that has a computer ask them if they use a programmer and why. Did it take the programmer a few hours or months to write their program?

 Tell Me More:
Association for Systems Management
24587 Bagley Rd.
Cleveland, OH 44138
http://www.iccp.org

The Association for Computing
1515 Broadway
New York, NY 10036

Computer Support Specialists and Database Administrators

 Education and Training:

Usually a bachelor's degree is necessary. More companies are also requiring certification.

 Job Outlook:

Excellent

Computer support specialists may work within an organization or for a software vendor.

 Average Earnings:

Medium

What They Do: Computer support specialists provide help and advise computer users. They help people with computer software and hardware problems. They often work for a company which publishes software or makes computers. Database administrators develop and maintain databases for a company. Databases are collections of information which is stored on a computer. A telephone number directory is a database. They coordinate changes to databases and also may be responsible for keeping the system secure.

Working Conditions: Computer support specialists and database administrators work in offices. They spend long periods of time in front of a computer.

Related Jobs: Computer engineer, computer scientist, computer programmer, financial analyst, urban planners, mathematician, statistician, operations research analyst, management analyst, and actuary

Subjects To Study Now and Later: Mathematics, chemistry, computers, physics and English

Getting Ready and Places to Go to Observe: If you have access to a computer, use it as much as you can. Learn about different types of software, from desktop publishing to database management programs. Read computer magazines to learn about different computers and hardware. There is a great amount of information on the internet if you have access to it.

 Tell Me More:

Association for Computing (ACM)
1515 Broadway
New York, NY 10036

Certification of Computing
  Professionals (ICCP)
2200 East Devon Ave., Suite 268
Des Plaines, IL 60018
http://www.iccp.org

Computer Systems Analysts

Education and Training:

A bachelor's degree and work experience are usually required. Graduate degrees are preferred.

Job Outlook:

Excellent

Average Earnings:

Medium

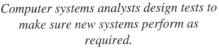

Computer systems analysts design tests to make sure new systems perform as required.

What They Do: Computer systems analysts use computers to learn about a company's problems. Computers are also used to help solve these problems. First, analysts learn about the problems and goals from the managers of the company. Then, using different methods, like engineering, mathematics, and accounting, the analyst plans what computer and software should be used to solve the problems and fulfill the goals of the company.

Working Conditions: Computer systems analysts work in comfortable offices. They usually work 40 hours a week.

Related Jobs: Computer programmer, financial analyst, urban planner, engineer, operations research analyst, management analyst, and actuary

Subjects To Study Now and Later: Mathematics, business, computer science, English, and physics

Getting Ready and Places to Go to Observe: Find a minor problem around your home or school, such as getting everyone to work and school on time. Try to find a solution to the problem, You can work out the problem on computer or on paper. How will you organize activities and people to resolve this problem? Contact a large company. Ask if they employ a computer systems analyst. If they do, contact that person to find out more about this job.

Tell Me More:
IEEE Computer Society,
    Headquarters Office
1730 Massachusetts Ave. NW
Washington, DC 20036-1992

Certification of Computing
    Professionals (ICCP)
2200 East Devon Ave., Suite 268
Des Plaines, IL 60018
http://www.iccp.org

Operations Research Analysts

 Education and Training:

A master's degree in computer science and a high level of computer skills are usually required.

Job Outlook:

Good

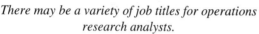

There may be a variety of job titles for operations research analysts.

 Average Earnings:

Medium - High

What They Do: Operations research analysts solve problems in large businesses. Computers are used to learn about these problems and to find ways to solve them. Some work only for certain types of businesses, such as airline companies. The problems may involve organizing, the production of goods, or a number of other matters.

Working Conditions: Operations research analysts spend most of their time sitting in a comfortable office. Work weeks may be more than 40 hours because of a client's needs. Many operations research analysts work for the military.

Related Jobs: Computer scientist, statistician, engineer, mathematician and economist

Subjects To Study Now and Later: Mathematics, computer science, business, English, and foreign languages

Getting Ready and Places to Go to Observe: Computers as a hobby is one way to begin preparing for this career. With computers you can also increase your math and writing skills. The local military office may have additional information about this job.

 Tell Me More:

Military Operations Research Society
101 South Whiting St., Suite 202
Alexandria, VA 22304

The Institute for Operations Research
& the Management Sciences
901 Elkridge Landing Rd., Suite 400
Linthicum, MD 21090

Education and Training:

Employers usually look for college graduates, but experience and knowledge is just as important.

Job Outlook:

Excellent

Webmaster is a fast-growing occupation serving the needs of small and large companies.

Average Earnings:

Medium - High

What They Do: Webmasters design and maintain websites. Their skills must continue to grow as companies and organizations are depending more on their websites to do business. Webmasters must have knowledge of computers, graphic design, programming, business, writing and marketing. Webmasters work with various departments, such as marketing, sales, and human resources in planning a website. Since this is such a new and growing field, the job will continue to change in the next few years.

Working Conditions: Webmasters work on a computer most of the time. Because of technology, webmaster jobs can often be done almost anywhere, including one's home.

Related Jobs: Computer programmer, graphic designer, computer scientist, marketing manager, computer engineer, and systems analyst

Subjects To Study Now and Later: Mathematics, computers, marketing, business, English, and graphic design

Getting Ready and Places to Go to Observe: If you have access to a web development program, practice designing a personal web page of your own. You don't even need internet access. When you are able to be on the world wide web, check the many different sites that offer support for webmasters. Read some of the internet magazines that are available.

Tell Me More:

Webmaster's Guild
http://www.webmaster.org

Association for Computing (ACM)
1515 Broadway
New York, NY 10036

Biological Scientists

Education and Training:
A bachelor's degree and often a master's degree or doctorate is required.

Many biological scientists work in laboratories.

Job Outlook:
Excellent

Average Earnings:
Medium

What They Do: Biological scientists study living things. They learn how cells, animals and beings relate to the world in which they live. Most work only in a certain area, such as ornithology, which is the study of birds. Some biological scientists' work is managing programs. Others consult for businesses, zoos and government. Increases in biological knowledge have created new jobs and fields.

Working Conditions: Most biological scientists work in offices, laboratories or classrooms. Some, such as zoologists, often work outdoors.

Related Jobs: Forester, range manager, soil conservationist, animal breeder, horticulturist, agricultural scientist, and medical scientist

Subjects To Study Now and Later: Biology, chemistry, mathematics, and English

Getting Ready and Places to Go to Observe: Curiosity is part of the biological scientist's way of life. Borrow books from the library for ideas on how to bring science into your home. Contact groups that arrange bird watching or nature walks. Read science magazines and articles. Camping, parks and natural museums are all good ways to get outdoors and learn about the biological world around you. Talk to a biology teacher about your interests to get ideas for projects to do on your own.

Tell Me More:

American Institute of Biological Sciences
1444 I St. NW, Suite 200
Washington, DC 20005
http://www.aibs.org

Education and Training:
A bachelor's degree is needed, and often a doctorate is required.

Job Outlook:
Good

Average Earnings:
Medium

What They Do: Foresters manage, plan and help protect forests. They plan how much wood and what type of wood is to be harvested. Foresters arrange with loggers for the removal and sale of the trees. Foresters also watch over the planting and growing of new trees after logging an area. Some may design campgrounds and manage parks.

Working Conditions: Foresters work in offices, but they often work outdoors in all kinds of weather. They may have to travel long distances by foot, car, plane or horse.

Related Jobs: Wildlife manager, agricultural scientist, biological scientist, soil scientist, environmental scientist, and ranch manager

Subjects To Study Now and Later: Biology, computer science, mathematics, communications, and English

Getting Ready and Places to Go to Observe: Write to groups, like the Sierra Club, that educate about forests. Get a papermaking kit to learn the basics of how paper is made. The library offers many books on trees and science. Camping, state parks and natural museums are all good ways to get outdoors and learn about the biological world around you. County and state fairs have exhibits that teach you about the land in your state.

Tell Me More:
Society of American Foresters
5400 Grosvenor Lane
Bethesda, MD 20814
http://www.safnet.org

Chief, U.S. Forest Service
US Dept. of Agriculture
PO Box 96090, SW
Washington, DC 20090-6090

Marine Biologists

Marine biologists may spend much of their time on the ocean.

 Education and Training:

A bachelor's degree is the minimum requirement. There are more opportunities for those with a doctorate degree.

 Job Outlook:

Good

 Average Earnings:

Medium - High

What They Do: Marine biologists study things that live in the ocean. The ocean covers a large part of the earth, so there are many things to learn from the life in the ocean. Marine biologists may study one type of species, such as a dolphin. Or they may study more than one species to learn how they interact with each other. Some marine biologists study life in the ocean to learn more about an entire ecosystem. Marine biologists also try to learn how organisms adapt to their water environment, such as how light affects the sea life.

Working Conditions: Marine biologists may spend some of their time in small or large research boats. They also spend time in a lab or office.

Related Jobs: Marine geologist, oceanographer, limnologist, aquatic scientist, underwater archaeologist, and aquatic veterinarian

Subjects To Study Now and Later: Biology, mathematics, statistics, computers, oceanography, English, and meteorology

Getting Ready and Places to Go to Observe: Read about your interests that are related to the ocean. Also, read about weather. If you can spend some time around the ocean, be aware of what you see. Observe changes that take place over a day, a week, or even a season. Write these observations down to document them.

 Tell Me More:
American Society of Oceanography
5400 Bosque Blvd., Suite 680
Waco, TX 76710-4446
http://www.aslo.org

National Aquarium in Baltimore
Educational Department, Pier 3
501 East Pratt St.
Baltimore, MD 21202-3120
http://www.aqua.org

Education and Training:

A bachelor's degree is needed. College teaching jobs normally require a doctorate.

Job Outlook:

Good

Average Earnings:

Medium - High

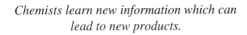

Chemists learn new information which can lead to new products.

What They Do: Chemists search for new, useful ways to use chemicals. Chemists have made many new products, such as paints, drugs and man-made fibers. They often work for manufacturing companies. There, chemists test and watch over the production of products. Often, chemists will specialize in a field, like biochemistry, which combines the study of biology with chemistry.

Working Conditions: Chemists work indoors in laboratories, manufacturing plants, or the classroom. Some may do part of their work outdoors, collecting samples for a study, for example.

Related Jobs: Chemical engineer, physicist, medical scientist, biological scientist, and chemical technician

Subjects To Study Now and Later: Biology, chemistry, mathematics, computer science, physics, and English

Getting Ready and Places to Go to Observe: Talk to your parents about home chemistry sets. Go to the library to read about inventors. Find someone with a computer who will help you learn how to use it. Local colleges and universities have chemistry departments that can provide more information about the use of chemicals.

Tell Me More:

American Chemical Society
Education Division
1155 16th St. NW
Washington, DC 20036

Geologists

Geologists determine the composition of rock specimens in laboratories.

 Education and Training:

A bachelor's degree and sometimes additional education are required.

 Job Outlook:

Good

 Average Earnings:

High

What They Do: Geologists study the earth and its history. They study rocks on the surface of the earth. Rocks below the earth's surface are studied by drilling deep into the earth. Geologists also review facts collected by satellites. Computers are used to study the fossils of animals and plants. Geologists search for oil, natural gas, underground water, and learn about earthquakes.

Working Conditions: Some geologists spend most of their time in offices, while others spend a lot of their time outside or in laboratories. Some travel is required. Work at field sites is common.

Related Jobs: Mathematician, engineering and science technician, petroleum engineer, surveyor, soil scientist, and mapping scientist

Subjects To Study Now and Later: Biology, chemistry, mathematics, computer science, and physics

Getting Ready and Places to Go to Observe: Start a rock collection. You can buy them from rock and gem stores, but finding them yourself is more fun. If your family camps, learn about the history of the area you'll be visiting. Contact groups which do nature hikes to learn about the areas around you. Contact the geology department of a local college. The teachers and students may be able to talk to you about this career.

 Tell Me More:
American Geological Institute
4220 King St.
Alexandria, VA 22302-1507
http://www.agiweb.org

Geological Society of America
P.O. Box 9140
Boulder, CO 80301
http://www.geosociety.org

Meteorologists

Meteorologists forecast the weather.

Education and Training:

A bachelor's degree is required for this job. Often, a doctorate degree is necessary.

Job Outlook:

Good

Average Earnings:

Medium - High

What They Do: Meteorologists study the air that surrounds the earth. They learn how the air affects the earth. By learning about the air, meteorologists have discovered ways to inform us about the weather. They also study air-pollution and changes in the earth's climate. Computers and satellites are used in their work.

Working Conditions: Meteorologists work indoors in offices. Those who forecast weather may work in small offices at all hours of the day and night.

Related Jobs: Oceanographer, geologist, hydrologist, and civil and environmental engineer

Subjects To Study Now and Later: Biology, chemistry, physics, mathematics, and computer science

Getting Ready and Places to Go to Observe: Keep track of the weather where you live. Try to get a barometer and outdoor thermometer. Record the daily high and low temperatures. Measure the rainfall. Compare the facts you collect with earlier years. Contact the local news stations in your area. Many of them hire meteorologists for weather reports. Ask if there is a good time to meet with the weather reporter. Your newspaper can tell you if there are local weather hobbyists near you. They usually enjoy sharing their knowledge.

Tell Me More:
American Meteorological Society
45 Beacon St.
Boston, MA 02108
http://www.ametsoc.org/AMS

Physicists

Most physicists work in research and development.

 Education and Training:
A doctorate is a normal requirement for physicists.

 Job Outlook:
Poor

 Average Earnings:
High

What They Do: Physicists study the forces of nature, such as gravity. They plan and perform experiments with lasers, telescopes, and other tools. Based on what they learn from these experiments, physicists will form ideas and laws to describe the forces of nature. Astronomy, which is a part of physics, is the study of the moon, stars, and all parts of the universe.

Working Conditions: Most work indoors in laboratories and offices at universities. Some may travel to work in distant places. When travelling, physicists often work at night.

Related Jobs: Chemist, geophysicist, engineer, computer scientist, and mathematician

Subjects To Study Now and Later: Physics, mathematics, computer science, astronomy, chemistry, and English

Getting Ready and Places to Go to Observe: Get a good astronomy book from the library and study the stars. You do not need a telescope to search the skies. While you are at the library, read other books about physics. A good understanding of advanced mathematics is important, so work on your mathematics skills. Contact the physics department of a local college or university. Ask them if you can have a tour of the labs. What research projects are they conducting?

 Tell Me More:
American Center for Physics
Career Planning & Placement
One Physics Ellipse
College Park, MD 20740-3843

http://www.aip.org

Lawyers are also called attorneys.

Education and Training:

This job usually requires at least three years of college before attending three years of law school. There is also a test, called a bar exam, which must be passed.

Job Outlook:

Good

Average Earnings:

High

What They Do: Lawyers represent people in court. They present arguments that support their clients. This job requires a lot of research and understanding of laws. They often use computers to help research and prepare cases and write reports. They also counsel clients about their legal rights.

Working Conditions: Lawyers do most of their work in offices, law libraries and courtrooms. This job requires lots of travel. They usually work long hours each week.

Related Jobs: Mediator, arbitrator, journalist, patent agent, title examiner, legislature assistant, and lobbyist

Subjects To Study Now and Later: English, social studies, mathematics, science, and computer operations

Getting Ready and Places to Go to Observe: Hold court in your family or classroom. You be the lawyer. Find out all the facts and prepare your case. Use witnesses and have them testify. The best place to see a lawyer at work is in the courtroom.

Tell Me More:

American Bar Association
541 North Fairbanks Court
Chicago, IL 60611

Law School Admission Council
P.O. Box 40
Newtown, PA 18940
http://www.isac.org

Paralegals

Paralegals do background work for lawyers.

 Education and Training:

Paralegals need to attend training programs that take two to four years to complete. Some paralegals train on-the-job.

 Job Outlook:

Excellent

 Average Earnings:

Medium

What They Do: Paralegals work with lawyers. They do research and check facts to help prepare cases for trial. They write reports and special legal papers, keep files and help the lawyer during a trial. Paralegals do a lot of the same work as a lawyer. Many paralegals use computers to help them in their job.

Working Conditions: Paralegals usually work 40 hours per week. They work inside at desks in offices and law libraries. Sometimes it is necessary to work longer hours to meet deadlines.

Related Jobs: Abstractor, claim examiner, occupational safety and health worker, police officer, and title examiner

Subjects To Study Now and Later: English, accounting, business, mathematics, word processing, and shorthand

Getting Ready and Places to Go to Observe: When you prepare a research paper for school you are doing some of the same things as a paralegal. Find out everything you can about a hobby or subject you enjoy and write a report that tells all the fats about that subject or hobby. Contact a law office in your area to talk to a paralegal and get more information about this job.

 Tell Me More:

Standing Committee on Legal Assistants
American Bar Association
750 North Lake Shore Dr.
Chicago, IL 60611

National Association of Legal Assistants, Inc.
1516 South Boston St., Suite 200
Tulsa, OK 74119
http://www.nala.org

Education and Training:

A bachelor's degree is needed for this job. Graduate training is sometimes required.

Job Outlook:

Good

Average Earnings:

Medium

What They Do: Economists research and study how society uses resources like raw materials, labor, land, and machinery that makes products. They use this knowledge to help advise businesses and government agencies. Some economists develop opinions about causes of inflation or recessions. Others analyze data on prices, wages, safety, health, and interest rates.

Working Conditions: Economists use calculators and computers. Sometimes they work alone, other times they work as a group. They work overtime if needed to meet deadlines. Travel is sometimes required.

Related Jobs: Financial manager, financial analyst, actuary, insurance underwriter, loan officer and budget officer

Subjects To Study Now and Later: Mathematics, social studies, computer science, foreign languages, English, and accounting

Getting Ready and Places to Go to Observe: Use books from the library to learn about wages, interest rates and recessions. Read the newspaper to find out what economists think about these items. Banks, insurance and government agencies in larger cities hire economists.

Tell Me More:

National Association of Business
  Economists
1233 20th St. NW, Suite 505
Washington, DC 20036

Marketing Research Association
2189 Silas Deane Hwy., Suite 5
Rocky Hill, CT 06067

Psychologists

Counseling psychologists advise people on how to deal with problems.

 Education and Training:

A master's or doctorate degree is needed for this career.

 Job Outlook:

Good

 Average Earnings:

Medium - High

What They Do: Psychologists study the way people think, feel and act. Counseling psychologists help people deal with problems about divorce, family, jobs, or growing older. They help mentally ill patients adapt to life. School psychologists help students with learning or behavior problems. There are several other types of psychologists.

Working Conditions: Psychologists work in offices at schools, clinics, and hospitals. They sometimes work evenings and weekends. Travel may be required.

Related Jobs: Public relations manager, clinical social worker, clergy, special education teacher, and counselor

Subjects To Study Now and Later: Social studies, mathematics, computer operations, English, sociology, and psychology

Getting Ready and Places to Go to Observe: Observe people around you. Do you see people helping other people with problems? Watch what they do to help solve the problem. Do you have ideas that would help? Visit the psychologist at your school. Your doctor can also tell you about a psychologist in your area.

 Tell Me More:

National Association of School
   Psychologists
4030 East West Highway, Suite 402
Bethesda, MD 20814

American Psychological Association
Research Office and Education in
   Psychology and Accreditation
   Offices
750 1st St., NE
Washington, DC 20002
http://www.apa.org

Urban and Regional Planners

Local government planning agencies employ urban and regional planners.

Education and Training:

A master's degree program in urban or regional planning and additional training are usually required.

Job Outlook:

Good

Average Earnings:

Medium

What They Do: Urban and regional planners develop programs that plan for growth and renewal of urban, suburban, and rural communities. They prepare reports about how the land is currently used and make suggestions about changes for the future on social, economic, and environmental issues. Computers are often used in this job.

Working Conditions: Urban and regional planners work inside in offices and outside studying the land and its current use. They often attend meetings during evenings and weekends.

Related Jobs: City manager, civil engineer, geographer, and architect

Subjects To Study Now and Later: English, computer operations, mathematics, and sociology

Getting Ready and Places to Go to Observe: Read about your area in the newspaper. Talk to adults about the changes that are taking place to learn if they are the result of rapid growth, environmental situations, or other reasons. Talk to people that have lived in the area a long time. How has the area has changed and why? While driving to and from your home during the week, watch for places that are under construction. Local government planning agencies hire urban and regional planners that can tell you more about this career.

Tell Me More:

American Planning Association
122 South Michigan Ave., Suite 1600
Chicago, IL 60630-6107

Recreation Workers

Recreation workers need strong leadership skills.

Education and Training:

The level of education for this career varies from a high school diploma to a bachelor's degree. Most supervisors have a bachelor's degree and work experience.

Job Outlook:

Good

Average Earnings:

Low

What They Do: Recreation workers plan, organize, and direct activities that people do in their spare time. They work in many areas like community centers, parks, campgrounds, schools, churches, and corporations. Recreation workers often give instruction in activities, teach classes, and plan and direct daily activities.

Working Conditions: Recreation workers work anywhere from a vacation cruise ship to a campground. This occupation requires working evenings and weekends.

Related Jobs: Recreational therapist, social worker, parole officer, school counselor, and teacher

Subjects To Study Now and Later: English, speech, physical education, computer operations, and mathematics

Getting Ready and Places to Go to Observe: Organize a fun day for family or friends. Plan the activities, put together the supplies, and direct the group. Places that have recreation workers are camps, cruise ships, local recreation departments, amusement parks, and after-school programs.

Tell Me More:

National Employee Services and
  Recreation Association
2211 York Rd., Suite 207
Oakbrook, IL 60521

National Recreation and
  Park Association
Division of Professional Services
2775 South Quincy St., Suite 300
Alexandria, VA 22206
http://www.nrpa.org

Social and Human Service Assistants

 Education and Training:

Most employers prefer some college background. Some employers hire only those with bachelor's degrees.

 Job Outlook:

Excellent

 Average Earnings:

Low

Social workers travel locally to visit clients.

What They Do: Social and human service assistants work under the direction of people from fields such as nursing, psychiatry, rehabilitation or social work. Their duties will vary depending on the field in which they work. For example, in rehabilitation settings, they may help someone perform everyday activities. In a nursing setting, they may assist patients with medications. Their responsibility and supervision will also vary. Some are on their own most of the time and others may have close supervision.

Working Conditions: Social and human service assistants' working conditions vary. While the work is mainly indoors, some may work in shelters, hospitals or offices. Others may spend their day visiting clients.

Related Jobs: Social worker, religious worker, occupational therapy assistant, physical therapy assistant, psychiatric aide and activity leader

Subjects To Study Now and Later: English, psychology, sociology, humanities, science

Getting Ready and Places to Go to Observe: Volunteer work is a good way to try to find out if this is the type of work for you. Your school counselor or someone at your church or temple may be aware of programs in which you can enroll. Look around you. Are there neighbors that could use your assistance?

 Tell Me More:

National Association of Human
    Service Education
Brookdale Community College
Luncroft, NJ 07738

Council on Standards in Human
    Service Education
Northern Essex Community College
Haverhill, MA 01830

Protestant Ministers

Many ministers are active in community projects.

 Education and Training:

Many religions require a bachelor's degree with additional religious education after college.

 Job Outlook:

Poor

 Average Earnings:

Medium

What They Do: Protestant ministers lead the members of their church in services and prayer. They perform marriages and conduct funerals. Protestant ministers also visit the sick and aged at home and in the hospital. Many people go to their minister for guidance when they have a personal problem. In churches with a lot of members, there may be staff to help the minister. Ministers are usually available for emergencies that involve members of their churches.

Working Conditions: Protestant ministers normally work indoors. Sometimes ministers must work long hours reading or writing sermons.

Related Jobs: Social worker, clinical and counseling psychologist, teacher, and counselor

Subjects To Study Now and Later: English, history, biology, sociology, psychology, art, music, religion, philosophy, and foreign languages

Getting Ready and Places to Go to Observe: Talk to the minister of the church in which you are involved. Ask questions such as what educational and training requirements are needed. Learn about the job duties the minister performs. What duties does the minister enjoy the most and least? Attend church services and activities. Observe the minister. Listen to what the minister says. Ask your minister, parents, and family questions that you may have about what the minister says during the service.

 Tell Me More:

Seek the counsel of a minister or church guidance worker.

Rabbis organize religious and educational programs for their congregations.

Education and Training:

A bachelor's degree and three to five years of additional schooling are required.

Job Outlook:

Excellent

Average Earnings:

Medium - High

What They Do: Rabbis are the leaders and teachers of the Jewish religion. Rabbis perform services, weddings, and conduct funeral services. They visit the sick, help the poor and guide members of their temple who have personal problems. In temples with a large membership, rabbis will work with staff who help with activities and various duties of the temple. Large temples may also have an assistant rabbi.

Working Conditions: Rabbis work indoors reading, writing, performing services, or community and educational activities. Long hours are worked since rabbis are usually available to temple members any time of the day or night for emergencies.

Related Jobs: Social worker, clinical and counseling psychologist, teacher, and counselor

Subjects To Study Now and Later: English, history, art, biology, music, religion, sociology, psychology, philosophy, and foreign languages

Getting Ready and Places to Go to Observe: Borrow books from the library about religion and history. Talk to a rabbi about Jewish customs. Ask questions about the rabbi's education. What does the rabbi like the most and the least about the job.

Tell Me More:

Rabbinical Council of America
305 7th Ave.
New York, NY 10001
(orthodox)

The Jewish Theological Seminary
of America
3080 Broadway
New York, NY 10027
http://www.jtsa.edu

Roman Catholic Priests

Priests visit and counsel parishioners.

Education and Training:

Becoming a priest usually requires eight years of study after high school.

Job Outlook:

Excellent

Average Earnings:

Low

What They Do: Roman catholic priests take care of the educational and religious needs of the members of their church. They perform services, weddings, and funeral services. Priests comfort the sick, assist the poor, and offer advice and support to people with personal problems. Diocesan priests usually work with elementary and high schools attached to a church. Religious priests do most of the teaching of the religion to people outside of the faith. Priests take a vow of poverty and are supported by the church.

Working Conditions: Long hours at all times of the day and night are worked by priests. Some move to other countries to help teach the religion to people from all over the world. Some priests spend many hours preparing sermons.

Related Jobs: Social worker, clinical and counseling psychologist, teacher, and counselor

Subjects To Study Now and Later: English, sociology, philosophy, biology, history, foreign languages, and religion

Getting Ready and Places to Go to Observe: Talk to a priest. Ask questions such as what educational and training requirements are needed. Learn about the job duties the priest performs. What does the priest enjoy most and the least about the job? Attend church services. Observe the priest and listen to what is said during the sermon.

Tell Me More:

Seek the guidance and counsel of parish priests and diocesan vocational office.

Curators plan and oversee the work of maintaining collections.

Education and Training:

A bachelor's or master's degree, and museum work experience are what employers look for when hiring.

Job Outlook:

Poor

Average Earnings:

Medium

What They Do: Curators are in charge of collections in museums, historic sites, zoos, and aquariums. They plan and prepare exhibits, research collections, purchase items and direct the affairs of the museum. Some curators specialize in one area, like botany or history.

Working Conditions: Curators have different job duties that include working with the public, working in an office, installing exhibits, and travelling.

Related Jobs: Arborist, botanist, historian, librarian, and zoologist

Subjects To Study Now and Later: English, art, chemistry, history, physics, and computer operations

Getting Ready and Places to Go to Observe: Look around your home for an item that looks very old. Ask questions about this item. Go to the library and do research about the value, how old it is, or from where it came. Write down your findings. Offer suggestions about preserving this item for future generations. Visit a museum or historical site. Some curators work with the public answering questions and will give you a lot of information about the museum and the job.

Tell Me More:

American Association of Museums
1575 I St. NW, Suite 400
Washington, DC 20005

Society of American Archivists
600 South Federal St., #504
Chicago, IL 60605

College and University Faculty

College and university faculty may give lectures to several hundred students.

 Education and Training:

A master's or doctorate degree is required depending on the college or university.

 Job Outlook:

Good

 Average Earnings:

Medium - High

What They Do: College and university faculty teach and advise college students. Faculty usually teach within one department based on one subject, such as mathematics or biology. They often teach several different classes within that subject. For example, a faculty member of the mathematics department might teach algebra and calculus classes. Faculty must keep up with new changes, ideas and knowledge within their field. Many must also do their own research to expand knowledge in their field.

Working Conditions: College and university faculty work flexible hours. During summer, they may have more time to travel or do research. Most work indoors, but some may work outdoors depending on their field.

Related Jobs: Elementary and secondary school teacher, librarian, writer, consultant, lobbyist, trainer and employee development specialist, and policy analyst

Subjects To Study Now and Later: English, social studies, mathematics, biology, and computer science

Getting Ready and Places to Go to Observe: Contact different colleges and universities. Tell them you are doing research and would like information on how they hire faculty.

 Tell Me More:

Contact the associations in the field in which you are interested. Some of them may be listed in this book.

American Association of University Professors
1012 14th St. NW, Suite 500
Washington, DC 20005

Many counselors work for schools and school districts.

 Education and Training:
A master's degree is usually needed for this career.

 Job Outlook:
Good

 Average Earnings:
Medium

What They Do: Counselors help people deal with problems and concerns about family, career, educational and personal matters. They also help people determine their interests, abilities, and disabilities. Many types of counselors include school and college, rehabilitation, employment and mental health.

Working Conditions: Counselors usually have separate offices to meet with people privately. Self-employed counselors also work some evenings and weekends. School counselors work the same hours as teachers.

Related Jobs: Teacher, human services worker, psychologist, psychiatrist, clergy, and occupational therapist

Subjects To Study Now and Later: English, social studies, mathematics, science, and computer operations

Getting Ready and Places to Go to Observe: Do you find that you are good at problem solving and helping people? Work on solving a special problem of your own. Most schools have counselors that can answer questions about this career.

 Tell Me More:

American Counseling Association
5999 Stevenson Ave.
Alexandria, VA 22304

National Board for Certified Counselors
3 Terrace Way, Suite D
Greensboro, NC 27403
http://www.nbcc.org

Elementary School Teachers

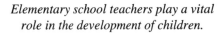

Elementary school teachers play a vital role in the development of children.

Education and Training:

Elementary school teachers usually need a bachelor's degree followed by a training program and certification.

Job Outlook:

Good

Average Earnings:

Medium

What They Do: Elementary school teachers educate children as they begin to learn about arithmetic, language, social studies, and science. They usually teach an entire class several subjects by giving lessons, tests, and special projects. Teachers also prepare lesson plans, grade papers and tests, fill out report cards, meet with parents, and attend meetings.

Working Conditions: Teachers work in classrooms most of the time. Some teachers have two months off during the summer. Other teachers work year around with week long breaks during the year.

Related Jobs: Preschool worker, librarian, social worker, and counselor

Subjects To Study Now and Later: English, mathematics, social studies, science, and computer operations

Getting Ready and Places to Go to Observe: If you are a classroom helper you are learning some of the things that teachers do in their jobs. Help someone learn something new. Your school is the best place to see teachers at work.

Tell Me More:

American Federation of Teachers
555 New Jersey Ave. NW
Washington, DC 20001

National Education Association
1201 16th St. NW
Washington, DC 20036

 Education and Training:

Most librarians have a master's degree.

 Job Outlook:

Poor

 Average Earnings:

Low - Medium

What They Do: Librarians perform many duties that make information available to the public. They work with people to help them find the information they need, they purchase and prepare new materials for use, and they manage the staff and activities of the library. Books are the main source for information. There are also a large amount of fiction books which are mainly read for pleasure. Magazines, newspapers, videos, and audio cassettes are also available at libraries.

Working Conditions: Some librarians work with people, others work at computers or desks. Public and college librarians often work evenings and weekends. School librarians work the same schedule as classroom teachers.

Related Jobs: Archivist, museum curator, research analyst, and records manager

Subjects To Study Now and Later: English, mathematics, computer operations, science, and social studies

Getting Ready and Places to Go to Observe: Visit your public and school library often. Observe the librarian at work. What kinds of jobs do you see the librarian doing? Ask about volunteering or helping with summer youth programs. Try and locate a special library or college library that you can tour. Ask your public librarian for information on the location of other libraries in your area.

 Tell Me More:

Special Libraries Association
1700 18th St. NW
Washington, DC 20009

American Library Association
Office for Library Personnel Resources
50 East Huron St.
Chicago, IL 60611
http://www.ala.org

Secondary School Teachers

Secondary school teachers lecture and demonstrate to students.

Education and Training:

A bachelor's degree and a certification program are necessary for this career.

Job Outlook:

Good

Average Earnings:

Medium

What They Do: Secondary school teachers instruct students in one specific subject or several related courses. They teach more detail about the basics learned in elementary school. Teachers need to continue their education throughout their career to be able to educate using the latest technology. Computers and videos may be used to help them teach. They plan and assign lessons, prepare tests, grade tests and papers, write report cards, and meet with staff and parents.

Working Conditions: Some teachers have two months off during the summer months. Other teachers work year around with week long breaks during the year.

Related Jobs: Counselor, librarian, sales representative, and social worker

Subjects To Study Now and Later: English, social studies, mathematics, science, and computer operations

Getting Ready and Places to Go to Observe: If you like one particular subject in school, study all you can about that subject. Find out why your teacher chose to teach. Visit your local high school to talk with secondary school teachers.

Tell Me More:

American Federation of
   Teachers
555 New Jersey Ave. NW
Washington, DC 20001

National Education Association
1201 16th St. NW
Washington, DC 20036

Special Education Teachers

Education and Training:

A bachelor's degree and often a fifth year of education is needed. Some states require a master's degree.

Job Outlook:

Excellent

Average Earnings:

Medium

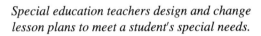

Special education teachers design and change lesson plans to meet a student's special needs.

What They Do: Special education teachers work with children and youth that have special needs. These needs can be various, including learning disabilities, mental retardation, speech or hearing impairments, autism and gifted and talented. Special education teachers will design a program to meet goals established for each student. Communication with parents, social workers, school psychologists, physical therapists and other teachers is often a large part of the job. Special education teachers are increasingly using specialized computers.

Working Conditions: Special education teachers usually work in a classroom at a school. Some work in a hospital environment or tutor students in their homes.

Related Jobs: School psychologist, social worker, speech pathologist, rehabilitation counselor, adapted physical education teacher, physical therapist, recreational therapist, and occupational therapist

Subjects To Study Now and Later: English, social studies, mathematics, and psychology

Getting Ready and Places to Go to Observe: Contact the district office for your school and ask to speak with a special education teacher. Try to visit their classroom. Be ready to ask questions about what they do during the workday, what materials they use, and what is the best way to prepare for their job.

Tell Me More:
National Clearinghouse for Professions in Special Education
Council for Exceptional Children
1920 Association Dr.   *http://www.cec.sped.org*
Reston, VA 20191

Chiropractors

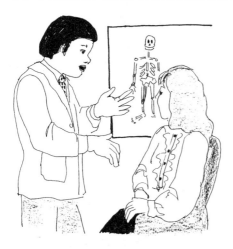

Chiropractors evaluate posture.

 Education and Training:

Two years of undergraduate study, four years of chiropractic courses, and taking a state exam are required to work in this career.

 Job Outlook:

Good

 Average Earnings:

High

What They Do: Chiropractors deal with muscular, nervous, and skeletal system problems. They examine the patient, take X-rays, perform tests and do a spinal analysis. They adjust the spinal column and use water, light, heat therapy, and ultrasound for treatment. They do not prescribe drugs or perform surgery. They encourage a healthy lifestyle.

Working Conditions: Chiropractors usually work in a group or in private practice. They often work evenings and weekends when clients are available.

Related Jobs: Physician, dentist, optometrist, podiatrist, veterinarian, and physical therapist

Subjects To Study Now and Later: English, physics, anatomy, chemistry, biology, mathematics, social studies, and computer operations

Getting Ready and Places to Go to Observe: Study about the skeletal system from books at the library. Local educational stores may have miniature plastic skeletons to look at. There are pamphlets available from local chiropractors that explain about disorders and proper treatment. Visit a local chiropractor and ask to see the type of equipment used. Find out what type of treatment is recommended for different injuries.

 Tell Me More:

American Chiropractic Association
1701 Clarendon Blvd.
Arlington, VA 22209

International Chiropractors
 Association
1110 North Glebe Rd., Suite 1000
Arlington, VA 22201

Education and Training:

Dentists need two years of college to attend dental school. Dental school takes three to five years to complete. Each state has tests that need to be passed before working.

Job Outlook:

Poor

Average Earnings:

High

Dentists play an important role in a persons's overall health.

What They Do: Dentists identify and take care of teeth, gum, and mouth problems. They pull teeth, perform surgery, fix broken or decayed teeth, and make molds for dentures and crowns. Dentists are also involved with preventive dental care. They teach people how to take care of their teeth by brushing, flossing, using fluoride and eating a proper diet. They use X-ray machines and hand tools like drills.

Working Conditions: Many dentists work at their own business. Their work hours may include evenings and weekends when patients can come in. Dentists wear gloves, masks, and safety glasses for protection against germs and disease.

Related Jobs: Clinical psychologist, optometrist, physician, veterinarian, and podiatrist

Subjects To Study Now and Later: English, chemistry, physics, biology, mathematics, and health

Getting Ready and Places to Go to Observe: Pay special attention to your own dental needs. Floss and brush regularly. When you are in the dentist office look for booklets that provide information about dental care. Let your dentist know of your interests. You may be able to watch your dentist working on another patient.

Tell Me More:

American Dental Association
Commission on Dental Accreditation
211 E. Chicago Ave.
Chicago, IL 60611

American Association of
Dental Schools
1625 Massachusetts Ave. NW
Washington, DC 20036
http://www.ada.org

Optometrists

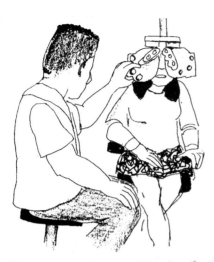

Many optometrists are self-employed.

Education and Training:

Two or three years of college are needed before attending four years at an optometry school to receive a Doctor of Optometry.

Job Outlook:

Good

Average Earnings:

Medium - High

What They Do: Optometrists treat vision problems and certain eye diseases. They examine a patient's vision by using instruments to test how to treat eye conditions, like prescribing glasses or vision therapy. Some optometrists work in special areas, such as sorts vision. Some teach and do research.

Working Conditions: Optometrists work in comfortable offices that are clean and have good lighting. They need to be exact with their hands and enjoy detail work. Some work evenings and Saturdays.

Related Jobs: Physician, dentist, chiropractor, podiatrist, and veterinarian

Subjects To Study Now and Later: English, physics, chemistry, biology, mathematics, and sociology

Getting Ready and Places to Go to Observe: Study pamphlets and material available from your optometrist or library. If you have not had an eye exam, then ask someone who had one to tell you about it and the treatment they needed. Your area has optometrists you can contact. They work in private practice, clinics, vision care centers, and retail optical stores.

Tell Me More:

American Optometric Association
Educational Services
243 North Lindbergh Blvd.
St. Louis, MO 63141-7881

Association of Schools and Colleges
of Optometry
6110 Executive Blvd., Suite 510
Rockville, MD 20852
http://www.opted.org

Education and Training:

Four years of college are required to attend medical school. It usually takes four years to complete medical school. After medical school, there are three to eight years of internship and residency.

Job Outlook:

Excellent

Average Earnings:

High

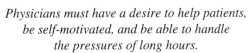

Physicians must have a desire to help patients, be self-motivated, and be able to handle the pressures of long hours.

What They Do: Physicians treat people's illnesses and injuries. They do tests that help them diagnose health problems. Physicians also counsel people on preventive health care. Some physicians, like pediatricians and family practitioners, are called primary care physicians. They see the same patients for different problems, like ear infections, measles, and a broken finger. Other physicians see patients for mainly one type of problem. Cardiologists, for example, see patients who need medical care for their heart.

Working Conditions: Physicians work in clinics and hospitals. They put in long hours depending on the patients needs. Some evening and weekend work is needed.

Related Jobs: Audiologist, chiropractor, dentist, optometrist, podiatrist, speech pathologist, and veterinarian

Subjects To Study Now and Later: English, chemistry, physics, biology, mathematics, social studies, and health

Getting Ready and Places to Go to Observe: When you go to your physician for an illness or injury, ask questions about the tests they do and the treatment you get. Do you know how they use the different equipment and supplies? What do they like about their job?

Tell Me More:

American Medical Association
515 N. State St.
Chicago, IL 60610

Association of American Medical
  Colleges, Section for Student
  Services
2450 N. St. NW
Washington, DC 20037-1131
http://www.aamc.org

Podiatrists

Podiatrists learn everything about the 26 bones which are in the foot.

Education and Training:

Podiatrists need to be a graduate of a college of podiatric medicine and pass examinations

Job Outlook:

Good

Average Earnings:

High

What They Do: Podiatrists identify and treat disorders and diseases of the foot and lower leg. They use X-rays and tests to help diagnose problems. They prescribe drugs, perform surgery, and order physical therapy. Some podiatrists specialize in areas like pediatrics or sports medicine.

Working Conditions: Podiatrists usually work in offices, hospitals, or clinics. Some work evenings and weekends.

Related Jobs: Chiropractor, dentist, optometrist, physician, and veterinarian

Subjects To Study Now and Later: English, physics, biology, chemistry, mathematics, health, and computer operations

Getting Ready and Places to Go to Observe: Books from the library will have more information on feet and bones. Ask your physician for the name of a podiatrist you can talk to in your area. Check the yellow pages for a complete list.

Tell Me More:

American Podiatric Medical Assoc.
1701 Clarendon Blvd.
Arlington, VA 22209
http://www.apma.org

American Assoc. of Colleges of
 Podiatric Medicine
1350 Piccard Dr., Suite 322
Rockville, MD 20850-4307
http://www.aacpm.org

Veterinarians

Many veterinarians own their own pet hospital or clinic.

Education and Training:

A Doctor of Veterinary Medicine degree, passing a state exam, and a national exam are needed to practice veterinary medicine.

Job Outlook:

Excellent

Average Earnings:

Medium

What They Do: Veterinarians diagnose and treat all kinds of animals. They give animals shots to prevent diseases, set broken bones, perform surgery, and prescribe medicine. Veterinarians teach owners about proper care and breeding. Some veterinarians work in research or as food safety inspectors. Others are livestock inspectors, and some care for zoo animals.

Working Conditions: Veterinarians work in pet hospitals or clinics. Those who treat large animals also travel to farms and ranches. They work long hours and some nights and weekends.

Related Jobs: Chiropractor, dentist, optometrist, physician, podiatrist, zoologist, and marine biologist

Subjects To Study Now and Later: English, chemistry, physics, biology, mathematics, social studies, and computer operations

Getting Ready and Places to Go to Observe: If you like taking care of animals and being around them you have two things in common with veterinarians. Offer to "pet sit" for neighbors or friends who are taking a vacation. Read about different kinds of animals and their needs. In your area visit veterinarian clinics, pet stores, and the zoo. Ask lots of questions about different needs of the animals.

Tell Me More:

American Veterinary Medical
    Association
1931 N. Meacham Rd., Suite 100
Schaumburg, IL 60173-4360

Association of American Veterinary
    Medical Colleges
1101 Vermont Ave. NW
Washington, DC 20005

Audiologists

Education and Training:

A master's degree, clinical experience, and passing a state exam are required for this career.

Audiologists use audiometers to measure the loudness at which a person begins to hear sounds.

Job Outlook:

Excellent

Average Earnings:

Medium

What They Do: Audiologists diagnose and treat people with hearing problems. They use special equipment to test a person's hearing. Audiologists work directly with patients and physicians when treating clients.

Working Conditions: Audiologists work indoors at a desk or table. Some travel is needed between treatment locations.

Related Jobs: Occupational therapist, speech-language pathologist, optometrist psychologist, and physical therapist

Subjects To Study Now and Later: English, mathematics, health, speech, and computer operations

Getting Ready and Places to Go to Observe: Learn all you can about how the ear works. Find out how a hearing aid is able to help people hear better. Audiologists work in special hearing clinics or in medical buildings. Ask your physician or school nurse about an audiologist in your area.

Tell Me More:

American Academy of Audiology
8201 Greensboro Dr., Suite 300
McLean, VA 22102

American Speech-Language-
Hearing Association
10801 Rockville Pike
Rockville, MD 20852
http://www.asha.org

Dietitians and Nutritionists

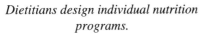
Dietitians design individual nutrition programs.

  Education and Training:

A bachelor's degree, a training program, and passing a national exam is needed for this career.

 Job Outlook:

Good

 Average Earnings:

Medium

What They Do: Dietitians and nutritionists plan nutritional programs for hospitals, schools, and nursing homes. They work with people to determine their nutritional needs and plan a healthy eating program. Dietitians sometimes counsel people with special problems like being overweight or diabetic. Some work as researchers or teachers.

Working Conditions: Dietitians work in clean areas that are well lighted. They sometimes work in large kitchens that can be hot. They may have to stand a lot.

Related Jobs: Home economist, food service manager, nurse, and health educator

Subjects To Study Now and Later: Biology, English, chemistry, health, home economics, mathematics, and communications

Getting Ready and Places to Go to Observe: Study about nutrition and plan a healthy meal for your family. If someone you know has special health needs, ask if they have a dietitian help them plan their meals. What do they eat that is different than what your family eats? Your school or district may have a dietitian with whom you can meet and find out more about how your school meals are planned. Nursing homes or hospitals in your area also employ dietitians.

 Tell Me More:

The American Dietetic Association
216 West Jackson Blvd., Suite 800
Chicago, IL 60606-6995
http://www.eatright.org

Occupational Therapists

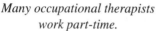

Many occupational therapists work part-time.

Education and Training:

A bachelor's degree and passing a national exam are needed for this career.

Job Outlook:

Excellent

Average Earnings:

Medium

What They Do: Occupational therapists work with people who have mental, physical, and developmental conditions that prevent them from working or living independent lives. Therapists help people learn everyday skills, like cooking or using a computer. They teach people how to use wheelchairs and devices that operate telephones and televisions. Occupational therapists must keep good records on their client's progress.

Working Conditions: Occupational therapists work in schools, hospitals, and some ravel to private homes. They work in rehabilitation centers that have machines and tools to make the job easier. This job requires lifting.

Related Jobs: Physical therapist, audiologist, rehabilitation counselor, and recreational therapist

Subjects To Study Now and Later: Biology, English, chemistry, physics, health, art, and social studies

Getting Ready and Places to Go to Observe: If you belong to a local youth group, join in when they do special projects that help people with special needs. Find out how old you need to be to volunteer at the hospital. Hospitals, schools, and nursing homes have occupational therapists at work.

Tell Me More:

American Occupational Therapy Association
4720 Montgomery Lane/PO Box 31220
Bethesda, MD 20824-1220
http://www.aota.org

Pharmacists

Education and Training:

It takes at least five years after high school to complete programs needed to get a degree required to become a pharmacist.

Pharmacists answer questions about prescription drugs.

Job Outlook:

Good

Average Earnings:

Medium

What They Do: Pharmacists administer drugs and medicines that physicians or other specialists prescribe. For safety reasons a computer keeps track of the amount of medicine given and the date it was purchased. Pharmacists also answer questions and give advice about the different kinds of drugs, their side effects, and the proper dosage.

Working Conditions: Pharmacists work in areas lined with shelves full of medicine. They stand most of the time and wear gloves and masks if needed for safety. They work evenings, weekends, and holidays if necessary.

Related Jobs: Medical scientist, pharmaceutical chemist, and pharmacologist

Subjects To Study Now and Later: English, physics, chemistry, biology, mathematics, social studies, and computer operations

Getting Ready and Places to Go to Observe: Study more about pharmacists by getting books from the library. If your doctor prescribes medicine for you, read the label that lists special directions from the pharmacist. How many important things are there to know about when taking that medication? Visit pharmacies that are located in hospitals, grocery, and drug stores in your area.

Tell Me More:

American Association of Colleges
 of Pharmacy
1426 Prince St.
Alexandria, VA 22314

Physical Therapists

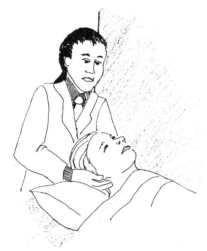

Physical therapists help people rehabilitate their injuries.

Education and Training:

A master's degree is recommended. All states require passing an exam before working as a physical therapist.

Job Outlook:

Excellent

Average Earnings:

Medium

What They Do: Physical therapists provide treatment and rehabilitation for people with injuries or diseases. After checking medical history and examining the patient they decide on a medical treatment plan. Physical therapists keep careful records. Some physical therapists work in many areas, others specialize in one area like pediatrics or sports physical therapy.

Working Conditions: Physical therapists work in schools, clinics, hospitals, and homes. They sometimes work evenings and weekends. This job requires lifting.

Related Jobs: Occupational therapist, speech pathologist, audiologist, and respiratory therapist

Subjects To Study Now and Later: Anatomy, English, biology, chemistry, social studies, mathematics, and physics

Getting Ready and Places to Go to Observe: If you enjoy working with others and have patience and understanding, you have some qualities needed to be a physical therapist. Older students can volunteer to work at a clinic or hospital.

Tell Me More:

American Physical Therapy Association
1111 North Fairfax St.
Alexandria, VA 22314-1488
http://www.apta.org/

Recreational Therapists

Recreational therapists help individuals build confidence through various activities.

 Education and Training:

A bachelor's degree in therapeutic recreation and an internship program are needed to work as a recreational therapist.

 Job Outlook:

Excellent

 Average Earnings:

Medium

What They Do:　Recreational therapists work with people that have illnesses or disabilities. They use activities like sports, games, and crafts to help people improve their health and medical problems. With information from the physician, patients, and family, the recreational therapist develops a program to improve the patient's health. They keep careful records about the patient's progress.

Working Conditions:　Recreational therapists work inside and outside. This job requires lifting people and equipment. They sometimes work evenings, weekends, and holidays.

Related Jobs:　Occupational therapist, music therapist, and rehabilitation counselor

Subjects To Study Now and Later:　English, chemistry, physics, biology, mathematics, and computer operations

Getting Ready and Places to Go to Observe:　Study more about recreational therapists with books from the library. If you like working with people and enjoy sports, dance, music, and games, you have some things in common with recreational therapists. Hospitals and homes for the elderly have recreational therapists employed.

 Tell Me More:

American Therapeutic Recreation
　Association
P.O. Box 15215
Hattiesburg, MS 39402-5215

National Therapeutic Recreation
　Society
22377 Belmont Ridge Rd.
Ashburn, VA 20148
email: NTRSNRPA@aol.com

Registered Nurses

Education and Training:

To get a nursing license, you must complete a two- to five-year nursing program.

Job Outlook:

Good

Average Earnings:

Medium - High

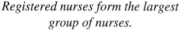

Registered nurses form the largest group of nurses.

What They Do: Registered nurses take care of sick and injured people. They help physicians with examinations. They provide treatment, dispense medication, monitor patients for symptoms and reactions, and keep careful records. There are many types of nurses, including hospital nurses, nursing home nurses, public health nurses, private duty nurses, and office nurses.

Working Conditions: Registered nurses work in hospitals, nursing homes, schools, and private homes. All nurses do a lot of walking, standing, and lifting.

Related Jobs: Occupational therapist, emergency medical technician, physical therapist, physician assistant, and respiratory therapist

Subjects To Study Now and Later: English, anatomy, chemistry, biology, mathematics, physiology, and nutrition

Getting Ready and Places to Go to Observe: The next time you go to your physician, watch the registered nurse at work. Ask questions about the kind of jobs that are done which the patient does not see. Ask to take a look at your chart to see how records are maintained. Hospitals, nursing homes, and physicians' offices all have registered nurses at work.

Tell Me More:

Communications Department
National League for Nursing
350 Hudson St.
New York, NY 10014

American Nurses Association
600 Maryland Ave. SW
Washington, DC 20024-2571

Respiratory Therapists

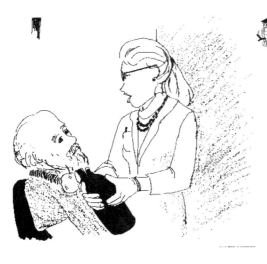

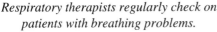

Respiratory therapists regularly check on patients with breathing problems.

Education and Training:

Most training programs are two years long. Some are four-year programs. Many hospitals require a special license.

 Job Outlook:

Excellent

 Average Earnings:

Medium

What They Do: Respiratory therapists treat and care for patients who have breathing problems. They treat all types of patients, including infants and the elderly. Respiratory therapists often use oxygen as treatment. They also use machinery to help the patient breathe. Respiratory therapists help a patient's family learn how to give treatment and use machinery properly at home.

Working Conditions: Respiratory therapists usually work in hospitals. Work weeks are 40 hours and may be days or nights. Respiratory therapists often work under great pressure.

Related Jobs: Registered nurse, physical therapist, occupational therapist, and radiation therapy technologist

Subjects To Study Now and Later: Health, biology, mathematics, English, chemistry, and physics

Getting Ready and Places to Go to Observe: Visit the library to borrow science and health care books. Talk to your doctor to learn more about how respiratory therapists work with infants and children. Find out how old you must be to volunteer in a hospital or nursing home. A visit to a hospital is one way to see respiratory therapists at work. Home health companies may have a respiratory therapist who will talk to you.

 Tell Me More:

American Association for
    Respiratory Care
11030 Ables Lane
Dallas, TX 75229

The National Board for
    Respiratory Care, Inc.
8310 Nieman Rd.
Lenexa, KS 66214

Speech-Language Pathologists

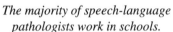
The majority of speech-language pathologists work in schools.

Education and Training:
A master's degree and training are needed for this career.

Job Outlook:
Excellent

Average Earnings:
Medium

What They Do: Speech-language pathologists prevent, diagnose, and treat speech and language disorders. They use written and oral tests to diagnose speech problems and recommend treatment. Speech-language pathologists work directly with patients and physicians when treating clients.

Working Conditions: Speech-language pathologists work indoors at a desk or table. Some travel is needed between treatment locations.

Related Jobs: Occupational therapist, physical therapist, and recreational therapist

Subjects To Study Now and Later: English, mathematics, physics, chemistry, biology, computer operations, health, and speech

Getting Ready and Places to Go to Observe: Use a tape recorder to record yourself and (with permission) two others in conversation. Listen carefully to the tape to hear if you notice any differences in the speech patterns. Books in the library can tell you about famous people with speech problems and the treatment or therapy they used. Your school or district employs a speech-language pathologist. Talk to the pathologist and find out more about this career.

Tell Me More:

American Speech-Language Association
10801 Rockville Pike
Rockville, MD 20852
http://www.asha.org/

Clinical Laboratory Technologists

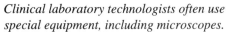

Clinical laboratory technologists often use special equipment, including microscopes.

 Education and Training:

A bachelor's degree is usually required.

 Job Outlook:

Good

 Average Earnings:

Medium

What They Do: Clinical laboratory technologists, also known as medical technologists, perform medical tests on blood, tissues and cells. These tests are important to learn what illness a person may have and how to treat it. Clinical laboratory technologists use microscopes, cell counters, and other special laboratory tools.

Working Conditions: Clinical laboratory technologists work indoors in clean laboratories. They stand a lot. They may have to work evenings, weekends, and holidays.

Related Jobs: Clinical technicians, food testers, veterinary laboratory technicians, analytical chemists, and science technicians

Subjects To Study Now and Later: Biology, chemistry, mathematics, English, and physics

Getting Ready and Places to Go to Observe: Read about biology and other sciences. Microscopes are interesting to use when looking at different things. With the supervision of an adult, you can also use books and kits to learn more about science. Hospitals hire clinical laboratory technologists. Ask your doctor's office if they run any medical tests at their office. Let them know of your interest and ask if you can watch them run tests.

 Tell Me More:

American Medical Technologists
710 Higgins Rd.
Park Ridge, IL 60068

American Society of Clinical
 Pathologists
Board of Registry
P.O. Box 12277
Chicago, IL 60612

Dental Hygienists

  Education and Training:

Two years of college is usually needed. A four-year or master's degree is required for some jobs, such as teaching.

 Job Outlook:

Excellent

 Average Earnings:

Medium

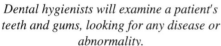

Dental hygienists will examine a patient's teeth and gums, looking for any disease or abnormality.

What They Do: Dental hygienists clean teeth. They also teach their patients how to take care of their teeth and mouth and keep them healthy. Dental hygienists take X-rays of the patient's mouth. Some states allow hygienists to do more of the same kinds of duties as a dentist. Dental hygienists work with small hand tools, X-ray machines, and medications.

Working Conditions: Dental hygienists wear safety glasses, masks, and gloves to protect themselves from illness. Hours worked may be part-time, full-time, and weekends.

Related Jobs: Dental assistant, podiatric assistant, office nurse, medical assistant, and physician assistant

Subjects To Study Now and Later: Biology, health, English, chemistry, psychology, speech, and mathematics

Getting Ready and Places to Go to Observe: It is important to be neat, clean, and in good health for this job. Learn to keep your own belongings clean and tidy. Keep your body and mouth healthy. Dental hygienists' fingers and hands must be steady. Do needlepoint, model building, or play the piano. Your own dentist's office is the best place to go to observe. Ask if there is time for them to show you the different instruments they use.

 Tell Me More:

Division of Professional Development
American Dental Hygienists' Association
444 N. Michigan Ave., Suite 3400
http://www.adha.org

Commission on Dental
 Accreditation
American Dental Association
211 E. Chicago Ave., Suite 1814
Chicago, IL 60611
http://www.ada.org

Dispensing Opticians

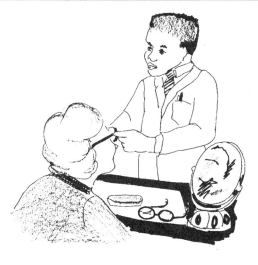

Dispensing opticians fit eyeglasses.

 Education and Training:

Some companies train on the job. Others require two-year degrees from a trade school or college.

 Job Outlook:

Good

 Average Earnings:

Medium

What They Do: Dispensing opticians help people choose frames for corrective eyeglasses. Usually, they work in a shop which makes the lenses, or they may work for an ophthalmologist or optometrist. Dispensing opticians order the laboratory work needed to make the eyeglasses. Then they make sure the finished eyeglasses fit the patient properly.

Working Conditions: Dispensing opticians work in shops which may have a laboratory where eyeglasses are made. 40-hour weeks are common, but some work less hours. They must stand a lot while working with patients.

Related Jobs: Jeweler, laboratory technician, locksmith, orthodontist, watch repairer, and ophthalmic laboratory technician

Subjects To Study Now and Later: Mathematics, science, English, physics, anatomy, and mechanical drawing

Getting Ready and Places to Go to Observe: It is very interesting to learn how eyes allow us to see. Go to the library to read about them. Visit stores in your area that sell eyeglasses. Sometimes you can watch the dispensing opticians at work.

 Tell Me More:

Opticians Association of America
10341 Democracy Lane
Fairfax, VA 22030-2521

National Academy of Opticianry
10111 Martin Luther King, Jr. Hwy.,
   Suite 112
Bowie, MD 20720-4299

EEG Technologists

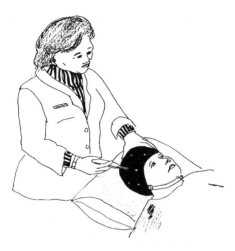

Most EEG technologists work in hospitals.

  Education and Training:

One- to two-year programs are offered after high school from some hospitals and colleges. Some EEG technologists learn their skills on the job.

 Job Outlook:

Excellent

 Average Earnings:

Medium

What They Do: EEG technologists give medical tests. They operate EEG (electroencephalograph) machines which record "brain waves". Some EEG technologists perform other tests which are also related to the brain. EEG technologists ask a patient about their medical history before giving tests. Sometimes, technologists give EEG's while a patient is having an operation.

Working Conditions: EEG technologists work in hospitals. They stand a lot of the time and may work with very ill patients. They may work evenings, weekends, and holidays.

Related Jobs: Radiologic technician, nuclear medicine technologist, and cardiovascular technologist

Subjects To Study Now and Later: Health, biology, mathematics, and English

Getting Ready and Places to Go to Observe: Read books about the brain. Scientists are learning more about it all the time. Hospitals are the most likely place to watch EEG technologists work. Call a local hospital to learn if it offers a teaching or research program. If so, ask if you can observe or get a tour to learn more.

 Tell Me More:

Joint Review Committee on Electroneurodiagnostic Technology Route 1, Box 63A Genoa, WI 54632

Executive Office American Society of Electroneurodiagnostic Technologists 204 W. 7th St. Carroll, IA 51401 *http://www.aset.org/*

Emergency Medical Technicians (EMT)

 Education and Training:

EMT's must have formal training after high school which takes less than a year to complete.

 Job Outlook:

Excellent

 Average Earnings:

Medium

Emergency medical technicians often deal with life-or-death situations.

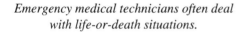

What They Do: Emergency medical technicians (EMT's) provide urgent and immediate medical care to people who have had an accident or are seriously ill. After giving medical care, they transport the ill or injured patient to a medical facility. EMT's often work in pairs and drive specially equipped emergency vehicles. Emergency medical technicians also give necessary information to the medical facility about the patient, replace supplies in the emergency vehicle, and check equipment.

Working Conditions: EMT's work indoors and outdoors. This job requires heavy lifting. Ambulance sirens may cause hearing loss. This is a stressful job caused from working with life-or-death situations.

Related Jobs: Police officer, firefighter, and air traffic controller

Subjects To Study Now and Later: English, health, mathematics, and science

Getting Ready and Places to Go to Observe: Television shows that relate true stories of emergency rescues show EMT's at work. Become CPR certified by attending a clinic provided by local health departments. Hospitals, police, fire, and health departments provide training for EMT's. Check with them to see if you can watch a training class.

 Tell Me More:

National Registry of Emergency
    Medical Technicians
P.O. Box 29233
Columbus, OH 43229

National Association of Emergency
    Medical Technicians
408 Monroe
Clinton, MS 39056

Health Information Technicians

Health information technicians make sure that medical records are complete and accurate.

 Education and Training:

A two-year degree is normally needed. Most employers prefer to hire accredited technicians, which requires passing a written test.

 Job Outlook:

Excellent

 Average Earnings:

Medium

What They Do: Health information technicians are responsible for making sure a patient's medical record is correct and complete. They work with doctors and other health workers to get additional facts needed for a patient's record. Some health information technicians are hired by hospitals, businesses, and law firms. They are hired to review records to gain knowledge which may help improve patient care or help lawyers working on a lawsuit.

Working Conditions: Health information technicians work indoors where many medical records are kept, such as hospitals. Some businesses, like law firms, hire them to review health information.

Related Jobs: Medical secretary, medical transcriber, medical writer, medical illustrator, and tumor registrar

Subjects To Study Now and Later: Biology, anatomy, physiology, mathematics, statistics, English, chemistry, health, and computer science

Getting Ready and Places to Go to Observe: Visit the library to borrow books related to science and health care. You may be able to buy a coloring book from an educational bookstore to help you learn the proper terms for parts of the body. Many different kinds of businesses hire medical record technologists. These businesses can be hospitals, nursing homes, law firms, insurance companies, and doctors' offices. Contact different businesses to learn how the job duties may change from one business to another.

 Tell Me More:

American Health Information Management Association
919 N. Michigan Ave., Suite 1400
Chicago, IL 60611
http://www.ahima.org

Nuclear Medicine Technologists

Education and Training:

Training programs are two to four years long. There are also Federal and state licensing requirements.

Job Outlook:

Poor

Average Earnings:

Medium

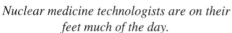

Nuclear medicine technologists are on their feet much of the day.

What They Do: Nuclear medicine technologists give medical tests similar to an X-ray to get a picture of the inside of a patient's body. Nuclear medicine technologists explain the test to patients and ask about their medical history. Nuclear medicine technologists operate the cameras that show the test results on film or a computer screen. Laboratories also hire nuclear medicine technologists to test blood.

Working Conditions: Nuclear medicine technologists work days, nights, and weekends. This job requires lifting. Special clothing is worn to prevent exposure to radiation.

Related Jobs: Radiologic, cardiovascular and EEG technologist, diagnostic medical sonographer, and respiratory therapist

Subjects To Study Now and Later: Biology, mathematics, physics, chemistry, computer science, and English

Getting Ready and Places to Go to Observe: Visit the library to borrow books related to science and health care. Find out how old you need to be to become a hospital volunteer. Hospitals are the best place to watch a nuclear medicine technologist at work. Also, contact a local college to see if they offer a program which leads to a career in nuclear medicine technology. The teachers and students may be able to talk to you.

Tell Me More:

The Society of Nuclear Medicine-
  Technologist Section
1850 Samuel Morse Dr.
Reston, VA 22090

Nuclear Medicine Technology
  Certification Board
2970 Clairmont Rd., Suite 610
Atlanta, GA 30329

Radiologic Technologists

  Education and Training:

Most training programs are one to four years

 Job Outlook:

Poor

 Average Earnings:

Medium

Radiologic technologists work at radiologic machines, but may also do some procedures at patients' bedsides.

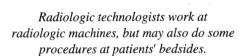

What They Do: Radiologic technologists operate equipment that makes X-ray films of the human body to find medical problems. They explain to the person how the X-ray is done. They also help cancer patients before and after they receive medication or radiation therapy. Medical doctors supervise the work of the radiologic technologist.

Working Conditions: Radiologic technologists work some evenings and weekends. This job requires a lot of standing and lifting. They work with machines in hospitals, vans, or doctor's offices.

Related Jobs: Nuclear medicine technologist, cardiovascular technologist and technician, perfusionist, respiratory therapist, and clinical laboratory technologist

Subjects To Study Now and Later: Mathematics, physics, chemistry, biology, English, and computer operations

Getting Ready and Places to Go to Observe: When you go to the doctor or dentist ask them about the radiologic technologist with whom they work. How do X-rays help them in their work? Ask to see an X-ray. Your hospital and dentist office are a great place to find out more about this job.

 Tell Me More:
American Society of Radiologic
  Technologists
15000 Central Ave., SE
Albuquerque, NM 87123-3917

Society of Diagnostic Medical
  Sonographers
12770 Coit Rd., Suite 708
Dallas, TX 75251

Surgical Technologists

Education and Training:

A two-year training program after high school is required.

Job Outlook:

Excellent

Average Earnings:

Medium

Surgical technologists spend much time cleaning medical instruments and setting up the operating room.

What They Do: Surgical technologists work in operating rooms. They help surgeons with operations. Before the operation they set up the equipment and instruments. Surgical technologists help during surgery by holding and passing instruments, counting supplies, and taking care of samples that need to go to the laboratory. After the operation they help take the patient to the recovery room.

Working Conditions: Surgical technologists normally work 40 hours a week. Sometimes they work on weekends or evenings. This job requires standing for several hours at a time.

Related Jobs: Licensed practical nurse, respiratory therapy technician, medical laboratory assistant, medical assistant, dental assistant, optometric assistant, and physical therapy aide

Subjects To Study Now and Later: Health, biology, chemistry, mathematics, and English

Getting Ready and Places to Go to Observe: Talk to someone you know who has had surgery. Do they remember how the surgical technologist helped them before or after the operation?

Tell Me More:

Association of Surgical Technologists
7108-C S. Alton Way
Englewood, CO 80112
http://www.ast.org/

Liaison Council on Certification for
the Surgical Technologist
7790 East Arapahoe Rd., Suite 240
Englewood, CO 80112-1274

Broadcast Technicians

Education and Training:

Training is available at technical schools and colleges. On-the-job experience and additional courses help technicians keep up with changing technology.

 Job Outlook:

Poor

 Average Earnings:

Low - Medium

Broadcast technicians must have manual dexterity and an ability to with electronic equipment.

What They Do: Broadcast technicians work with electronic equipment used to record and transmit radio and television programs. They install, service, and operate the equipment. Television cameras, tape recorders and transmitters are some of the equipment broadcast technicians operate.

Working Conditions: Broadcast technicians work in many places from network studios to natural disaster sites. This job requires climbing and heavy lifting. Many broadcast technicians work evenings, weekends, and holidays.

Related Jobs: Drafter, engineer and science technician, and air traffic controller

Subjects To Study Now and Later: Mathematics physics, electronics, English, and computer science

Getting Ready and Places to Go to Observe: Building electronic equipment from hobby kits or operating a "ham" radio are good ways to experience some of the jobs that are performed by broadcast technicians. Radio and television stations hire broadcast technicians. Local colleges sometimes have radio stations that you can visit. Stores that sell electronic hobby kits can answer questions about the technology broadcast technicians need to know.

 Tell Me More:

Society of Broadcast Engineers
8445 Keystone Crossing, Suite 140
Indianapolis, IN 46240

National Association of Broadcasters
  Employment Clearinghouse
1771 N St. NW
Washington, DC 20036

Public Relations Specialists

 Education and Training:

A college degree and public relations experience are recommended for this career.

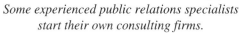

Some experienced public relations specialists start their own consulting firms.

 Job Outlook:

Good

 Average Earnings:

Medium

What They Do: Public relations specialists use media, like television and newspapers, to let people know positive information about the company or organization they represent. Sharing good information helps build a positive relationship between a company and the public. Public relations specialists also work for governments, universities, hospitals, and other organizations.

Working Conditions: Public relations specialists work various schedules that often include evenings and weekends. This job requires travelling.

Related Jobs: Advertising manager, lobbyist, police officer, fundraiser, and promotion manager

Subjects To Study Now and Later: English, advertising, psychology, speech, political science, and computer operations

Getting Ready and Places to Go to Observe: Television and newspapers have press releases, special reports, and news stories written by public relations specialists. Pick a local business, or make one up, and write a positive story about it. Writing for a school newspaper is good experience for this job. Public relations specialists often work behind the scenes. They work in hospitals, religious organizations, universities, and advertising agencies.

 Tell Me More:

Public Relations Society of America
33 Irving Place
New York, NY 10003-2376

The Society for Health Care
  Strategy and Market Development
One North Franklin St., Suite 31005
Chicago, IL 60606

Radio and Television Announcers

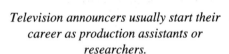

Television announcers usually start their career as production assistants or researchers.

Education and Training:

Most training programs are one to four years.

Job Outlook:

Poor

Average Earnings:

Medium - High

What They Do: Radio announcers introduce music, present news, sports, commercials, and interview guests. Television announcers present news stories and videotaped or live-transmission news. Some announcers specialize in sports or weather. Radio and television announcers must have a pleasant and well-controlled voice, excellent pronunciation, and correct English usage. This job is rewarding because it allows one to be creative and to become widely known.

Working Conditions: Announcers work unusual hours like early morning or late at night. They work indoors in soundproof rooms.

Related Jobs: Interpreter, producer, public relations specialist, actor, and teacher

Subjects To Study Now and Later: English, speech, drama, communications, electronics, and foreign languages

Getting Ready and Places to Go to Observe: Performing in front of an audience in talent shows or theater productions and any other type of public speaking gives you helpful experience for this type of job. Learn as much as you can about sports, music, politics, and the world around you. Visit a radio or television station near you. Colleges have campus radio stations and some areas have broadcasting schools that may give you a tour.

Tell Me More:

Broadcast Education Association
1771 N. St. NW
Washington, DC 20036

American Sportscasters Association
5 Beekman St., Suite 814
New York, NY 10038

Reporters

Education and Training:

A bachelor's degree and sometimes a master's degree are needed for this occupation. Experience working on a school newspaper or in a broadcasting station is helpful.

Job Outlook:

Good

Average Earnings:

Low - Medium

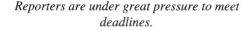

Reporters are under great pressure to meet deadlines.

What They Do: Reporters write stories for newspapers, television, and magazines. They collect facts and information on local, state, national, and worldwide events. They research, investigate, and interview people. Some reporters only cover specialized fields like politics, sports, or business.

Working Conditions: Reporters work indoors in offices and outside travelling to cover stories at the scene. Work hours change depending on deadlines and emergency stories.

Related Jobs: Writer, public relations worker, editor, educational writer, and biographer

Subjects To Study Now and Later: English, journalism, social studies, economics, and computer operations

Getting Ready and Places to Go to Observe: Writing stories for a school newspaper is a good way to gain experience. Using a computer helps with other needed skills. Contact your local newspaper and ask for a tour of the plant. Read your local newspaper and any other newspaper you can get your hands on. Read! Read! Read!

Tell Me More:

The Newspaper Guild
Research and Information Dept.
8611 Second Ave.
Silver Spring, ME 20910

Association for Education in
Journalism and Mass
Communications
University of South Carolina
LeConte College, Room 121
Columbia, SC 29208-0251

Writers

Education and Training:

A degree is usually needed. Some writing requires a good amount of knowledge in a certain field, such as engineering.

Job Outlook:

Good

Average Earnings:

Medium

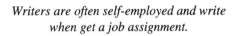
Writers are often self-employed and write when get a job assignment.

What They Do: Writers speak to people by writing about ideas and information. They create original writings for books, magazines, newspapers, advertising, radio and television. Writers may work independently or they may be hired by companies. Writers often research information to help them with their writing.

Working Conditions: Writers work in offices. They may travel to gather facts. Some overtime may be required to get a writing job completed on time.

Related Jobs: Newspaper reporter, radio and television announcer, advertising worker, and journalism teacher

Subjects To Study Now and Later: English, history, geography, and social studies

Getting Ready and Places to Go to Observe: Read as much as you can. Take a newspaper article and rewrite it in your own words. Write a story about an event that happened in your town. Keep a journal or diary. Write your own short stories. Volunteer to work on your school newspaper. The library has many books to borrow and read at home. Write to your local newspaper and explain your interest in being a writer. Ask if you can talk to a writer.

Tell Me More:

The Dow Jones Newspaper Fund
P.O. Box 300
Princeton, NJ 08540

American Society of
  Magazine Editors
919 3rd Ave.
New York, NY 10022

Designers

Creativity is important in all design occupations.

 Education and Training:

A high school diploma is usually needed for floral designers. Other designers, such as those who work with furniture and clothes will need two to four years of college.

 Job Outlook:

Good

 Average Earnings:

Low - Medium

What They Do: Designers arrange things or create products to look nice. Designers usually work with specific products such as flowers, clothes, movie sets, or furniture. Sometimes designers must create many drawings of new ideas to show to businesses or people who hire them. Computers are being used more often to create and illustrate a product.

Working Conditions: Some designers work for or own design companies. They have many clients. Others may design for just one company.

Related Jobs: Visual artist, architect, landscape architect, engineer, photographer, and merchandise displayer

Subjects To Study Now and Later: Art, woodworking, home economics, computer courses, and floristry

Getting Ready and Places to Go to Observe: Drawing, tracing, painting or sewing at home helps you create new ideas. Read weekly news magazines to learn about trends. Arrange your bedroom furniture in a new way, sew your own clothing, or draw a new design for a car. Go to art shows. Visit design companies in your town. Talk to art or design teachers and students at a local college about your interests. Ask if you can see some of the designs.

 Tell Me More:

National Association of Schools of
 Art and Design
11250 Roger Bacon Dr., Suite 21
Reston, VA 20190

Industrial Designers Society of
 America
1142-E Walker Rd.
Great Falls, VA 22066
http://www.idsa.org

Photographers

Photographers may work long and irregular hours.

 Education and Training:

Entry level jobs require at least a high school education. Some jobs, such as a photojournalist, require a bachelor's degree.

 Job Outlook:

Poor

 Average Earnings:

Medium

What They Do: Photographers use cameras to take photos of people, places, things, and events. They use special equipment, like different lenses and lights, to control how the pictures will look. Most send their film to laboratories to develop and print. Some develop and print their own photographs. As a type of art, photography allows someone to be creative, but it requires skill and knowledge. Photographers usually work in a specific field. Some of these fields are wedding photography, newspaper photography, and advertising photography.

Working Conditions: Photographers may work indoors and outdoors. They may need to work nights or travel.

Related Jobs: Illustrator, designer, painter, sculptor, and photo editor

Subjects To Study Now and Later: Mathematics, physics, chemistry, art, business, and English

Getting Ready and Places to Go to Observe: Be creative with your own camera. Take photographs of different kinds of things and people. Check your local library for magazines or newsletters about photography. Join the school yearbook class as a photographer. Visit a local camera store to see all the different types of cameras available. A camera store should know of camera clubs that can give you more information.

 Tell Me More:

Professional Photographers of
   America
57 Forsyth St., Suite 1600
Atlanta, GA 30303

American Society of Media
   Photographers
14 Washington Rd., Suite 502
Princeton Junction, NJ 08550-1033

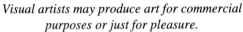

Visual artists may produce art for commercial purposes or just for pleasure.

Education and Training:

Training and schooling is recommended after completing high school. Community colleges and universities offer courses and degrees in various areas of art.

Job Outlook:

Poor

Average Earnings:

Low - Medium

What They Do: Visual artists use watercolors, pencils, clay, computers, or just about anything to create something, like a picture. These images may look realistic, or they may look vague and different, which is called abstract. Visual artists generally fall into one of two groups: graphic artists and fine artists. Graphic artists usually create images for businesses, stores, publishing companies and advertising firms. Fine artists often create art for their personal need to express themselves. Their work may be displayed in homes or art galleries.

Working Conditions: Visual artists generally work indoors in office buildings or in their homes. They need good lighting.

Related Jobs: Architect, display worker, floral designer, industrial designer, landscape architect, and photographer

Subjects To Study Now and Later: Art classes of all kinds, photography, computer graphics, and English

Getting Ready and Places to Go to Observe: You can experiment at home creating your own images. Find out what your parents will allow you to use. It can be pens, pencils, wood carvings, paint, ink, clay, play dough, or whatever your imagination tells you. Look at advertisements in magazines to see the different images graphic artists created using photos, paints, computers, and other things. Visit museums and art galleries. Some art galleries and museums will have someone who can explain how the artist made art pieces.

Tell Me More:

The National Association of
  Schools of Art & Design
11250 Roger Bacon Dr., Suite 21
Reston, VA 20190

The American Institute of
  Graphic Arts
164 5th Ave.
New York, NY 10010

Actors and Actresses

The glamour associated with acting attracts many people.

 Education and Training:

Experience from taking part in high school and college plays, local theaters and acting groups is helpful before starting formal training at dramatic art schools, colleges or universities.

 Job Outlook:

Poor

 Average Earnings:

Low - High

What They Do: Actors and actresses entertain and perform for people by memorizing a script and pretending they are the person whose role they are acting. They use costumes, props, and makeup to help. Some actors and actresses are "extras" and have no speaking parts. Other actors and actresses also teach acting courses.

Working Conditions: Actors and actresses work long hours and often travel. They work evenings and weekends. This job is stressful because performances need to be perfect and there can be long waits and lots of auditioning between jobs.

Related Jobs: Dancer, choreographer, disc jockey, radio and television announcer, and drama coach

Subjects To Study Now and Later: Drama, speech, dance, music, English, foreign languages, and physical education

Getting Ready and Places to Go to Observe: Gain experience by taking part in local theater groups, school plays, music or chorus groups, and modeling. Talk to the drama teacher at your school about acting. Local and regional theaters may let you sit in on a rehearsal to learn more.

 Tell Me More:

Screen Actors Guild
5757 Wilshire Blvd.
Los Angeles, CA 90036-3600

Theater Communications Group, Inc.
355 Lexington Avenue
New York, NY 10017

Dancers

Dancers must have a great deal of discipline.

 Education and Training:

Training and practice for dancers start at an early age and continues throughout the career. Private teachers, regional ballet schools, colleges, universities, and major ballet companies provide training.

 Job Outlook:

Poor

 Average Earnings:

Medium

What They Do: Dancers perform by moving their body and feet back and forth in rhythm. Types of dancing include ballet, modern, folk, ethnic, and jazz. Dancers may perform either in a group or by themselves. Some dancers sing and act. You will also find dancers that teach dancing. Some dancers, called choreographers, create new dances.

Working Conditions: Dancers rehearse for long hours each day including weekends and holidays. Travel is often required. Many performances are in the evening and on weekends. Dancers perform in front of people.

Related Jobs: Ice skater, dance critic, dance instructor, and dance therapist

Subjects To Study Now and Later: English, music, dance, physical education, literature, history, and art

Getting Ready and Places to Go to Observe: Training with a local dance teacher and performing in yearly dance productions is good experience in this field. Join school activities that require speaking or performing before an audience. Serious training for this occupation often begins by age 12. Attend dance performances in your area or region. Visit local dance schools and watch a rehearsal. Join in your school's talent show or musical production for more experience.

 Tell Me More:

National Association of Schools
   of Dance
11250 Roger Bacon Dr., Suite 21
Reston, VA 20190

The National Dance Association
1900 Association Dr.
Reston, VA 20190

Directors and Producers

 Education and Training:

Experience is often started in college plays and small theater groups. It takes many years to learn how to do the job well and to build a good reputation.

 Job Outlook:

Poor

 Average Earnings:

Medium - High

Directors interpret plays or scripts in bringing a show to an audience.

What They Do: Directors and producers are involved in the behind-the-scenes work of a show. Directors audition actors for performances in play, movies and radio shows. They run the rehearsals. Directors also manage the work of the cast and all the other people who are part of putting together a show. They are usually responsible for approving scenery, costumes, choreography and music. Producers are the business people who hire the director and manage the budget of the show. They will coordinate the activities of the writers, directors and managers.

Working Conditions: Directors and producers work either in offices or wherever the performance is taking place. They often work under stress. There may be travel.

Related Jobs: Actor, dancer, choreographer, costume designer, scriptwriter, company manager, booking manager, and playwright

Subjects To Study Now and Later: Communication, speech, drama, English, business, mathematics

Getting Ready and Places to Go to Observe: Read plays and scripts that you can find in the library. There are often interviews with directors and producers in entertainment publications and the newspaper. Many directors and producers started as actors. Learning what you can about the entertainment industry will be helpful.

 Tell Me More:

Association of Independent
    Video and Filmmakers
302 Hudson St., 6th Floor
New York, NY 10013

Educational Theatre Association
3368 Central Parkway
Cincinnati, OH 45225
Email: *pubs@one.net*

Musicians

Musicians begin studying at an early age.

 ## Education and Training:

Many musicians start studying at an early age. Even after completing high school and college, a musician continues training to work on improving skills.

 ## Job Outlook:

Poor

 ## Average Earnings:

Low - High

What They Do: Musicians perform one or more jobs. They may play a musical instrument, sing, write music, teach, or conduct vocal or instrumental performances. Some musicians perform alone, others in a group. Some performances are before a live audience. Other performances are recorded for television, radio, or movies.

Working Conditions: Musicians practice and rehearse often. Many musicians perform at night and on weekends. This job often requires travel. Many musicians work part-time in this occupation and also have jobs in other occupations.

Related Jobs: Songwriter, music critic, music therapist, music teacher, and disc jockey

Subjects To Study Now and Later: English, music, drama, dance, and theater

Getting Ready and Places to Go to Observe: Performing with a local theater group, joining the school or church choir, or being involved in school drama activities can you gain the experience needed to perform for audiences. Whether you play an instrument or sing, it is important to practice as much as possible. Entertainment provided by musicians can be found in many places. Visit your school choir or band while they are practicing. Check your newspaper for entertainment listings coming soon.

 Tell Me More:

National Association of
  Schools of Music
11250 Roger Bacon Dr., Suite 21
Reston, VA 20190

Professional Athletes

Professional athletes sometimes have problems with injuries.

  Education and Training:

Many attend college to get additional training and experience. Education is important, since an athlete's career is usually only a few years. More than 12 years of on-the-job training is usually required.

 Job Outlook:

Poor

 Average Earnings:

 Low - High

What They Do: Professional athletes compete in sporting events. They can be players on a team, such as baseball or basketball. Or, they can be in a sport where athletes compete alone against other people with the same skill, such as golf. On days when not playing or competing, athletes must still do physical exercises, practice, and continue to train. They usually have coaches and managers to guide them.

Working Conditions: Athletes work almost everyday to stay in good physical condition. They may work outdoors or indoors, depending on the sport. The time of year and length of time they compete varies.

Related Jobs: Sport coach, manager, umpire, and referee

Subjects To Study Now and Later: Physical education, health, psychology, history, and English

Getting Ready and Places to Go to Observe: Do a physical activity everyday. Watching sporting events is a good way to learn the rules and techniques of a game or sport, but playing yourself is the best way to learn. Good sportsmanship is also an important part of the athletic event. Education is critical for athletes. Reading, learning, and doing your best in school is important for an athlete's future.

 Tell Me More:

Write to your favorite teams of the sports you most enjoy playing. Also contact local colleges to learn of their sports program.

National Collegiate Athletic
   Association
NCAA Publishing
P.O. Box 7347
Overland Park, KS
http://www.ncaa.org

Umpires, Coaches and Referees

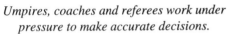

Umpires, coaches and referees work under pressure to make accurate decisions.

 Education and Training:

A great deal of knowledge of a sport is needed, as well as over one year of on-the-job training. Many coaches were former athletes.

 Job Outlook:

Good

 Average Earnings:

Medium

What They Do: Coaches, umpires and referees work with professional athletes and at sporting events. A coach helps athletes improve their skills. This can range from improving an athlete's technique by teaching a skill to emotional support. Umpires and referees judge a sporting event to make sure rules are followed. There is a lot of pressure placed on umpires and referees to have correct judgement when ruling on a play or timing in a sport.

Working Conditions: Coaches, umpires and referees spend a lot of time either outdoors or indoors, depending on the sport. There may be a lot of travel.

Related Jobs: Professional athlete, manager

Subjects To Study Now and Later: Physical education, health, nutrition, psychology, history, anatomy, and English

Getting Ready and Places to Go to Observe: Play a variety of sports to find the ones you enjoy the most. You can attend different sporting events at your local high school or community college and observe the coaches, umpires and referees. Watch the events as though you were the coach or umpire. Would you handle the sporting event differently than what you are observing? Read as much as you can about your sport of interest.

 Tell Me More:

Major League Baseball Umpire Development Program
P.O. Box A
201 Bayshore Dr. SE
St. Petersburg, FL 33731

http://www.minorleaguebaseball.com/udp

Marketing and Sales Occupations

Workers in this job cluster sell goods and services. Their educational training varies depending on the industry and the job. There should be a strong growth in employment for many of the jobs in this cluster.

Cashiers

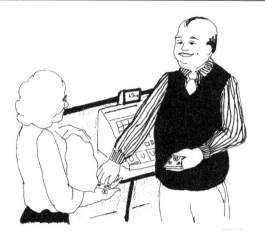

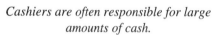
Cashiers are often responsible for large amounts of cash.

Education and Training:

A high school diploma is recommended. On-the-job training is often provided.

Job Outlook:

Excellent

Average Earnings:

Low

What They Do: Cashiers are in charge of the sale of goods. They total bills, receive money or checks, make change, fill out charge forms and give receipts. Supermarkets, stores, theaters, and food places all hire cashiers. Cash registers or computers with scanners are normally used to figure the amount of the sale. Cashiers also help with other jobs like stocking shelves and answering questions.

Working Conditions: Cashiers work with people. They work indoors and stand behind counters, or in booths. They can work up to 40 hours each week, but some cashiers only work part-time. Many cashiers work nights, weekends, and holidays.

Related Jobs: Food counter clerk, bank teller, counter and rental clerk, postal service clerk, and sales clerk

Subjects To Study Now and Later: English, mathematics, speech, computer operations, and bookkeeping

Getting Ready and Places to Go to Observe: Help out at a family or neighborhood garage sale. Mark the items with a price and help set up tables to show off the goods. Add up each purchase, collect money and make change. Almost every place you shop has a cashier. From gas stations to ice cream shops you'll see many different cashiers. What activities do they all do that are the same? Look in newspapers for cashier ads that list job duties and wages. Contact local businesses for more information about cashiers.

Tell Me More:

National Retail Federation
325 7th St. NW, Suite 100
Washington, DC 20004
http://www.nrf.com

International Mass Retail Association
1700 N. Moore St., Suite 2250
Arlington, VA 22209-1998

Financial Services Sales Representatives

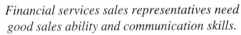

Financial services sales representatives need good sales ability and communication skills.

 Education and Training:

A college education is usually required.

 Job Outlook:

Excellent

 Average Earnings:

Medium

What They Do: Financial services sales representatives help people buy or sell stocks, bonds, and other financial products. They are also called brokers. They help customers with questions about investing money and understanding stock market terms. They spend a lot of time on the telephone finding new customers. Computers are used to help them with their job.

Working Conditions: Financial services sales representatives work in offices and also out of the office with clients. They usually work during normal business hours. Some evening and weekend work is needed.

Related Jobs: Insurance agent and real estate agent

Subjects To Study Now and Later: English, speech, mathematics, computer operations, accounting, and economics

Getting Ready and Places to Go to Observe: Check your newspaper for a list of stocks and their worth. Have someone explain to you how the stock market works or read a book about the stockmarket from the library. Pick a stock to watch everyday for one week. Figure out how much the stock would cost you if you bought ten shares. See how much money ten shares are worth one week later. Libraries have books that list representatives in different states.

 Tell Me More:

Contact personnel departments of individual securities firms. You can look them up in the yellow pages or on the web.

Insurance Agents

Most insurance agents work in small offices.

Education and Training:

A high school diploma with sales experience is the minimum for this career. A college education is preferred and necessary from some companies. All states require a license.

Job Outlook:

Poor

Average Earnings:

Medium

What They Do: Insurance agents help people and businesses select insurance policies. They advise about policies for health, automobiles, homes, and properties. These policies financially protect the client from losses like accidents, fire, or theft. Insurance agents sell many types of insurance.

Working Conditions: Insurance agents work in offices and often travel nearby to meet with people. They may work evenings and weekends.

Related Jobs: Real estate agent, broker, sales engineer, estate planning specialist, and financial advisor

Subjects To Study Now and Later: English, mathematics, speech, computer operations, and economics

Getting Ready and Places to Go to Observe: Talk to your family about the type of insurance that they have. Contact the insurance agent that helped them learn about the different types of policies. Other local insurance companies have insurance agents that can tell you more about this career.

Tell Me More:

Independent Insurance Agents
    of America
127 South Peyton St.
Alexandria, VA 22314

National Association of Professional
    Insurance Agents
400 N. Washington St.
Alexandria, VA 22314

Manufacturers' Sales Representatives

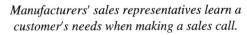

Manufacturers' sales representatives learn a customer's needs when making a sales call.

 Education and Training:

A high school and a college degree are recommended for this career. Many companies have training programs for new employees.

 Job Outlook:

Good

 Average Earnings:

Medium

What They Do: Manufacturers' sales representatives market products to wholesale and retail businesses. They explain about the good qualities of their products and the excellent service provided. Manufacturers' sales representatives also take orders and handle complaints.

Working Conditions: Manufacturers' sales representatives travel a lot. Some may work away from home for days or weeks at a time.

Related Jobs: Retail sales worker, real estate sales worker, insurance sales worker, and retail buyer

Subjects To Study Now and Later: English, speech, mathematics, computer operations, and bookkeeping

Getting Ready and Places to Go to Observe: Become involved in youth groups. This will help your skills in working with people. Fundraising projects use similar skills to those used by a representative. In large companies, like grocery stores, there are representatives who make sales calls to the manager. Can you think of other large businesses in your area that buy large amounts of products and probably have sales representatives who make sales calls to them?

 Tell Me More:

Manufacturers' Agents National
    Association
P.O. Box 3467
Laguna Hills, CA 92654-3467

Sales & Marketing Executives
    International
Statler Office Tower, Suite 977
1127 Euclid Ave.
Cleveland, OH 44115
http://www.smei.org

Real Estate Agents

Real estate agents spend much time showing property to clients.

 Education and Training:

A real estate agent must be a high school graduate. There are additional classroom instruction requirements and written tests which must be passed.

 Job Outlook:

Good

 Average Earnings:

Low - Medium

What They Do: Real estate agents help customers sell and purchase property. They help with the negotiations between buyer and seller. Many real estate agents work independently and are paid a commission when the real estate is sold. Agents need to know all the information available about the housing and commercial property industry in their community.

Working Conditions: Real estate agents work inside in offices and outside showing clients real estate for sale. This job requires working some evenings, weekends, and holidays.

Related Jobs: Motor vehicle sales worker, insurance agent, broker, and manufacturers' sales representatives

Subjects To Study Now and Later: English, mathematics, economics speech, computer operations, and bookkeeping

Getting Ready and Places to Go to Observe: Read the real estate section of the newspaper to study more about real estate in your region and how property is promoted. Compare prices, sizes and locations of homes. Look for ads with photos of real estate agents and the real estate they have listed for sale. As you drive to and from your home look for real estate signs that list property for sale.

 Tell Me More:

National Association of Realtors
Realtor Information Center
430 North Michigan Ave.
Chicago, IL 60611

The Appraisal Foundation
1029 Vermont Ave., NW, Suite 900
Washington, DC 20005-3517

Retail Sales Workers

Retail sales workers must be able to communicate clearly with customers.

 Education and Training:

There are no formal educational requirements for this job.

 Job Outlook:

Poor

 Average Earnings:

Low

What They Do: Retail sales workers sell products. Their main job is to interest people in buying goods. They also figure the sales slip, collect cash or checks, make change, write charge slips, bag the sold items, and give the paid slip to the buyer. They also help mark the price on goods, stock shelves, and take inventory.

Working Conditions: Retail sales workers stand a lot of the time. They usually work indoors. Some work evenings and weekends. Holidays are busy times and retail sales workers usually work long hours.

Related Jobs: Managers in wholesale trade, hotels, banks, and hospitals

Subjects To Study Now and Later: English, speech, mathematics, computer operations, bookkeeping, and economics

Getting Ready and Places to Go to Observe: Help your family or neighborhood with a garage sale. Mark items and set them out. Watch for shoppers that may have questions or need information about the products. When you make a sale, add up the prices, collect the money, and give change. Go shopping at retail stores to find retail sales workers doing their job. Look for differences in their behaviors, techniques and working conditions.

 Tell Me More:

National Retail Foundation
325 7th St. NW, Suite 1000
Washington, DC 20004
http://www.nrf.com

International Mass Retail
  Association
1700 N. Monroe St., Suite 2250
Arlington, VA 22209-1998
http://www.imra.org

Services Sales Representatives

Skill and knowledge are important for good communication between services sales representatives and their clients.

 Education and Training:

A college degree is usually required. Some companies have training programs.

 Job Outlook:

Excellent

 Average Earnings:

Medium

What They Do: Services sales representatives sell many kinds of services. They need to know all about the service they are selling and to be able to explain it to buyers. They answer questions, make visits, call, and write to customers to try and convince them to purchase the service. Once a sale is made they call on the buyers to see if the service met their needs and if they know anyone else that may want the service.

Working Conditions: Services sales representatives work in different ways. Some travel a lot and some work by using the telephone and sitting at a desk all day. Many set their own work hours and meet with buyers when it is a good time for them.

Related Jobs: Real estate agent, insurance agent, securities sales representative, retail sales worker, and travel agent

Subjects To Study Now and Later: English, mathematics, speech, computer operations, and bookkeeping

Getting Ready and Places to Go to Observe: Ask an adult about telephone calls or letters from services sales representatives they have received. What are they selling? Does a representative visit if they want to know more about the service?

 Tell Me More:

Sales and Marketing Executives
   International
66000 Hidden Lake Trail
Brecksville, OH 44141

National Retail Foundation
325 7th St. NW, Suite 1000
Washington, DC 20004
http://www.nrf.com

Travel agents often work long hours.

Education and Training:

Travel agents need special training for this job. Many vocational schools and some colleges offer training classes.

Job Outlook:

Excellent

Average Earnings:

Low

What They Do: Travel agents make travel plans for people. They buy tickets and help arrange travel times by checking into airline, bus, ship, and train schedules. They give advice on hotels, car rentals and tours. Travel agents answer customer questions and use computers to find out information that helps people make travel plans.

Working Conditions: Travel agents use computers and work inside at a desk. During holiday and vacation times they often work long hours.

Related Jobs: Meeting planners, tour guide, airline reservation agent, rental car agent, and travel counselor

Subjects To Study Now and Later: Mathematics, business, foreign languages, computer operations, history, geography, English, and speech

Getting Ready and Places to Go to Observe: Just for fun ask a friend where they would like to go on vacation. Plan out all the details like it was a real vacation. Get out a map and find the place they would like to go. Is the best way to get there by boat, plane, train, or car? If they fly what airports would they use? Local travel agents make travel plans for people everyday. Ask if you can watch them at work.

Tell Me More:
The Institute of Certified Travel
  Agents
148 Linden St./P.O. Box 812059
Wellesley, MA   02181-4282
(800) 542-4282

American Society of Travel Agents
Education Dept.
1101 King St.
Alexandria, VA   22314
*http://www.astanet.com/www/astnet/
whatis/becomeag.html*

Administrative Support Occupations

This cluster includes jobs that usually only require a high school diploma. The pay is also usually in the low range. Companies will train for many of the jobs listed. Important subjects to take in school are often English, mathematics, computers, and business courses.

Bank Tellers

Bank tellers often handle large sums of money.

 Education and Training:

A high school diploma is usually required. Some banks provide additional classroom instruction.

 Job Outlook:

Good, especially part-time jobs, because of high turnover.

 Average Earnings:

Low

What They Do: Bank tellers take care of financial needs of customers. Some of the jobs they do are cash or deposit checks, process loan paperwork and payments, and handle certificates of deposit and other transfers of money. Bank tellers are responsible for large sums of money. They must be careful to avoid errors.

Working Conditions: Bank tellers stand for long periods of time. There is full-time and part-time work available in this career. Evening and weekend work is sometimes needed.

Related Jobs: Cashier, post office clerk, toll collector, and ticket seller

Subjects To Study Now and Later: English, mathematics, computer operations, bookkeeping, and accounting

Getting Ready and Places to Go to Observe: Working with money is a good way to learn about the job that tellers do. Save as much money as you can for one month. Count your money and keep a list of how much you have. Start or add to a savings account. Check your bank book to be sure the money you put in the bank is the same as your list shows. Local banks often give tours to customers. It is fun to go inside the bank safe.

 Tell Me More:

American Bankers Association
1120 Connecticut Ave. NW
Washington, DC 20036

Bill Collectors

Education and Training:

A high school diploma is required. Companies usually train new bill collectors.

Job Outlook:

Excellent

Bill collectors spend much of their time talking on the telephone.

Average Earnings:

Low

What They Do: A bill collector's main responsibility is to collect payment on overdue bills. Bill collectors may use letters to first notify the customer. The telephone is often used to call and talk to the customer to try and work out an arrangement to pay the bill. If a customer cannot be found, the collector contacts the post office, neighbors, credit bureaus and relatives to try to find a new address for the customer. They sometimes disconnect services or start the process to take back the goods on which payments are owed, such as a car.

Working Conditions: Bill collectors work indoors in offices. They spend most of their time sitting down, talking on the telephone, and often work in front of a video display terminal.

Related Jobs: Customer service representative, telemarketer, and telephone interviewer

Subjects To Study Now and Later: Mathematics, English, psychology, foreign languages, public speaking, and typing

Getting Ready and Places to Go to Observe: Speaking well is an important part of this job. Listen carefully to what others say and what you say. Can you hear when someone is confident? What makes someone confident? How can a person be confident, but remain polite and courteous. Listen to yourself speak. Do you use proper grammar? In what ways can you improve your speech? There are bill collecting companies in many towns and cities. You can find listings in your local yellow pages. Talking to a bill collector at work can be very helpful in learning about this job.

Tell Me More:

American Collectors Association, Inc.
4040 West 70th St.
P.O. Box 39106
Minneapolis, MN 55439-0106

http://www.collector.com/consumer/careers.html

Billing Clerks

Invoices of charges to a customer are prepared by billing clerks.

 Education and Training:
Most jobs require at least a high school diploma.

 Job Outlook:
Good

 Average Earnings:
Low

What They Do: Billing clerks write and mail bills to customers showing the amount of money a customer owes to the business. Billing clerks get the information to write bills depending on the type of business for which they work. In some businesses, billing clerks review the orders and any shipping information. In hospitals, billing clerks review hospital records to figure how much to bill a patient. Many billing clerks use computers.

Working Conditions: Billing clerks work indoors. They sit for long periods of time. Many also work in front of a video display terminal.

Related Jobs: Bank teller, statistical clerk, receiving clerk, medical record clerk, credit clerk, hotel and motel clerk, and reservation and transportation ticket agent

Subjects To Study Now and Later: Mathematics, English, typing, and business education courses

Getting Ready and Places to Go to Observe: Work for your family for a day. Pretend that you are going to be paid. At the end of the day write a bill for the work that you have done. List all the jobs and the price you are charging for each chore. Look at other bills to see the way they are written. Hospitals and other large businesses are good places to go to see a billing clerk at work. Ask your family or a neighbor if there are billing clerks where they work.

 Tell Me More:

Association of Record Managers and Administrators (ARMA)
4200 Somerset Dr., Suite 215
Prairie Village, KS 66208

Education and Training:

A high school diploma is usually required.

Job Outlook:

Good

Average Earnings:

Low

Many brokerage clerks use video display terminals in their work.

What They Do: Brokerage clerks work for companies that sell and buy stocks, bonds, and other kinds of investments. There are many job duties a brokerage clerk may do that are related to the record keeping of these companies. Some match orders from people that want to buy a stock with orders from people that want to sell a stock. Others are responsible for making dividend payments on time. There are many possible duties of a brokerage clerk .

Working Conditions: Brokerage clerks work indoors in comfortable offices. They usually sit for long periods of time. Many also sit in front of a video display terminal.

Related Jobs: Statement clerk, accounting clerk, auditing clerk, bank teller, statistical clerk, receiving clerk, medical record clerk, and credit clerk

Subjects To Study Now and Later: Mathematics, English, typing, and business

Getting Ready and Places to Go to Observe: Read magazines and newspapers that tell about stocks and their worth. Have an adult explain how the stock market works. There are brokerage firms in most communities. Try to find the closest one to you. Find out if the brokerage firm will allow you to visit and show you around their office.

Tell Me More:

Association of Record Managers and Administrators (ARMA)
420 Somerset Dr., Suite 215
Prairie Village, KS 66208

Claim Representatives

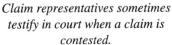

Claim representatives sometimes testify in court when a claim is contested.

  Education and Training:
A college degree is usually required.

 Job Outlook:
Good

 Average Earnings:
Medium

What They Do: Claim representatives work at insurance companies. They handle a policyholder's claim for damage or loss to something that is insured. The claim representative may be called an adjuster, examiner or investigator. They make sure the customer's insurance policy covers what is being claimed or lost. Claim representatives take pictures, interview witnesses, review police and hospital records, and prepare reports of what they learn.

Working Conditions: Most work indoors in offices. Some work outside the office, travelling to meet with customers or to the scene of a fire or disaster.

Related Jobs: Cost estimator, budget analyst, and investigator

Subjects To Study Now and Later: English, mathematics, computer operations, foreign languages, biology, and public speaking

Getting Ready and Places to Go to Observe: Ask your parents if they have ever filed an insurance claim. Ask for details or if you can see the report filed by the claim representative. Insurance sales representatives can be very helpful in telling you about the many duties of a claim representative.

 Tell Me More:

Insurance Information Institute
110 William St.
New York, NY 10038

Alliance of American Insurers
1501 Woodfield Rd., Suite 400 West
Schaumburg, IL 60173-4980

Clerical Supervisors and Managers

Clerical supervisors and managers communicate between clerks and professional technicians.

Education and Training:

Most firms promote from within the company. Many companies look for an associate's or a bachelor's degree, as well as work experience.

Job Outlook:

Good

Average Earnings:

Medium

What They Do: Clerical supervisors and managers are responsible for keeping offices running smoothly. They do this in many ways. They may oversee repairing broken equipment. Some are involved in the interviewing, hiring and training of employees. A clerical supervisor and manager must make sure the scheduling of employees' work hours cover absences due to illness or vacation. They are also the ones who evaluate a worker's performance. Clerical supervisors are often the people who communicate between the clerical staff and the managerial staff.

Working Conditions: Clerical supervisors and managers work in clean, comfortable offices. Most work a standard 40-hour week. Some may have to work various shifts since supervision is sometimes needed round-the-clock.

Related Jobs: Accounting clerk, cashier, bank teller, telephone operator and other manager positions

Subjects To Study Now and Later: Mathematics, computers, keyboarding, and English

Getting Ready and Places to Go to Observe: Almost all offices have supervisors or managers for their clerical staff. Anytime you go to an office, observe what the workers are doing and look for the person who may be the supervisor. Does the supervisor seem to know the job of the person for whom they are responsible?

Tell Me More:

State employment service offices can provide information about earnings, hours and employment opportunities in this and other clerical jobs.

Credit Clerks

A credit clerk reviews information a person provides about their credit and finances.

 Education and Training:

A high school diploma is preferred. Most credit clerks are trained on the job. Some take courses in credit from banks, vocational schools, colleges, and universities.

 Job Outlook:

Good

 Average Earnings:

Low

What They Do: Credit clerks collect facts to decide if someone should be accepted for credit. Credit is a way to buy something now and pay for it later. It is also a way to borrow money to be paid back later. They review loan forms and contact businesses and people for more information. They use this information to decide if people will have the money to pay back the loan.

Working Conditions: Credit clerks work indoors in comfortable offices. They sit for long periods of time. They also talk on the telephone a great deal.

Related Jobs: Credit authorizer, claim examiner and adjuster, customer-complaint clerk, procurement clerk, probate clerk, and collection clerk

Subjects To Study Now and Later: Typing, computer operations, bookkeeping, mathematics, and English

Getting Ready and Places to Go to Observe: Pretend you are borrowing $100. Figure out how you would pay back the money by making payments for 12 months. Most department stores hire credit clerks. Go to the credit department and ask them if they have a few minutes to talk to you to find out more about this career.

 Tell Me More:

Contact banks and credit institutions for information about credit clerks.

Dispatchers keep records of the calls they receive and the action they take.

 Education and Training:

A high school diploma is preferred. Some states require a special training program for public safety dispatchers.

 Job Outlook:

Good

 Average Earnings:

Low

What They Do: Dispatchers direct the movement of different types of vehicles. Some dispatchers, called public safety dispatchers, send a police car, fire truck or ambulance to an emergency. When they take a call, they carefully ask questions to learn about the emergency. The dispatcher quickly sends the correct service to help the caller. Truck dispatchers work for trucking companies. They direct the pickup and delivery of freight. There are dispatchers for trains, taxis, busses, tow trucks, and other types of services using vehicles.

Working Conditions: Dispatchers work indoors sitting for long periods. Most spend a lot of time at a computer screen. Some work nights, weekends, and holidays.

Related Jobs: Telephone operator, airline dispatcher, air traffic controller, transportation agent, and radio and television transmitter operator

Subjects To Study Now and Later: English, mathematics, physical education, typing, filing, computer operations, and first-aid training

Getting Ready and Places to Go to Observe: Talk to your family about who you call in an emergency. Who will respond to a fire or health emergency call? Some communities have one dispatching office for all emergency services. Contact your local police and fire stations to learn where their dispatcher works. Ask if you can observe the dispatcher at work for a short period of time. You can also contact local trucking companies and towing services.

 Tell Me More:

Association Public Safety
  Communication Officers
2040 S. Ridgewood
South Daytona, FL 32119-2257

National Academy of Emergency
  Medical Dispatchers
139 East South Temple, Suite 350
Salt Lake City, UT 84111

File Clerks

File clerks often use computerized filing systems.

 Education and Training:

A high school diploma is usually required.

 Job Outlook:

Poor

 Average Earnings:

Low

What They Do: File clerks keep files organized. They make sure a file folder is properly marked and coded so it is easy to identify. File clerks place files in their proper place, remove them when needed, and update information in files. If files can not be found, the file clerk must search for them. Some file clerks use equipment that takes a picture of the papers that go into file folders. This picture is stored on microfiche or computer disks. To retrieve information stored this way, the file clerk uses a computer or microfiche reader.

Working Conditions: File clerks work indoors in comfortable offices. Many must stoop, bend, reach and stand on their feet a lot. Some may sit in front of a video display terminal.

Related Jobs: Bank teller, billing clerk, receiving clerk, hotel and motel clerk, credit clerk, order clerk, brokerage clerk, and medical record clerk

Subjects To Study Now and Later: Mathematics, English, typing, and business

Getting Ready and Places to Go to Observe: Develop your own filing system with your homework. An old box can be used for filing. You can arrange the papers in alphabetical order, or you can file them in order of the date you did the homework. Look around your home to see what else would be easier to find if put in some kind of order. Spices used for cooking are one idea. Hospitals and other large businesses are good places to go to watch a filing clerk. Ask your family or friends if there are filing clerks where they work.

 Tell Me More:

Association of Record Managers and Administrators (ARMA)
4200 Somerset Dr., Suite 215
Prairie Village, KS 66208

General Office Clerks

Because they are so versatile, general office clerks find work in almost every type of business.

Education and Training:

A high school diploma is usually required.

Job Outlook:

Poor

Average Earnings:

Low

What They Do: General office clerks have different duties depending on the needs of the person for whom they work. Some of the common things they do are typing, filing, answering telephones, and delivering messages. They may use calculators, prepare mailings, keep records, or answer questions. Because they do so many things, general office clerks find work in all industries.

Working Conditions: General office clerks normally work indoors. Many work part-time hours.

Related Jobs: Cashier, medical assistant, teacher aide, and food and beverage service worker

Subjects To Study Now and Later: Typing, computer operations, bookkeeping, mathematics, and English

Getting Ready and Places to Go to Observe: Find ways to help out at home by doing some of the duties of a general office clerk. Answer the telephone and take messages for your family. Set up a filing system for the household bills and paperwork. Many offices, even your doctor's, will have a general office clerk at work. Watch for other businesses that hire general office clerks.

Tell Me More:

State employment service offices and agencies specializing in finding jobs for administrative support personnel can provide information.

Information Clerks

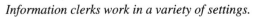
Information clerks work in a variety of settings.

Education and Training:

A high school diploma is usually required. Airlines prefer some college education. Most training is on-the-job.

Job Outlook:

Excellent

Average Earnings:

Low

What They Do: Information clerks gather information from the public. They also provide information by answering questions. Some information clerks check in guests at hotels and motels. They greet and direct customers on where to go for their special needs. They work in many places, like hospitals, businesses, airports or amusement parks.

Working Conditions: Since many information clerks actually see customers and visitors, work spaces must look nice. Information clerks may work indoors or outdoors. Some work nights and weekends. Many work part-time hours.

Related Jobs: Security guard, bank teller, guide and usher, lobby attendant, dispatcher, and telephone operator

Subjects To Study Now and Later: Mathematics, English, foreign languages, geography, history, psychology, public speaking, typing, and computer operations

Getting Ready and Places to Go to Observe: Since information clerks talk to people they have never met before, they must be friendly. You can work at being polite, friendly and pleasant to your family, friends, and new people you meet. Airports, amusement parks, shopping malls, large office buildings, and hotels usually employ information clerks. Information clerks answer the telephone when you call for schedule information for the busses in your community.

Tell Me More:

State employment offices can provide information about information clerk jobs.

Library assistants help people who want to borrow books.

Education and Training:
A high school diploma is the minimum education required.

Job Outlook:
Good

Average Earnings:
Low

What They Do: Library assistants work under the direction of librarians and help keep the library in order. This makes it easier for people to use the library. After getting necessary information, library assistants issue library cards to new library users. They record who borrows material and stamps the due date on the material being borrowed. They check due dates, sort returned material, and return it to the shelf. They answer questions. Some library assistants specialize in helping people that have sight problems, including blindness.

Working Conditions: Library assistants work indoors in libraries. They stoop, reach and spend a lot of time standing. Library assistants that work in schools often work only during the school year.

Related Jobs: Bookmobile driver, accounting clerk, auditing clerk, bank teller, statistical clerk, receiving clerk, medical record clerk, and credit clerk

Subjects To Study Now and Later: Mathematics, English, literature, and typing

Getting Ready and Places to Go to Observe: Read a lot. Learn the Dewey decimal classification system which is used in most libraries to organize books. Spend as much time as you can in the library. You can easily watch the library assistants and the librarian as they work. Talk to your school library assistant as well as a public library assistant. Find out what the differences are between working with the public and working with students.

Tell Me More:

The State Library of Ohio
Field Operations Department
65 South Front St.
Columbus, OH 43215

Mail Carriers

Even with new equipment, mail carriers must still sort some mail by hand.

Education and Training:

Mail carriers must pass a written and physical exam. They are trained on the job.

Job Outlook:

Poor

Average Earnings:

Medium

What They Do: Mail carriers deliver mail to businesses and homes. Most have an assigned route which they cover by foot, vehicle or both. They also collect mail from mail boxes on the street, or at businesses and homes on their route. Mail carriers also collect money when a letter does not have enough postage on it. Some mail requires that the mail carrier get a signature before it is delivered.

Working Conditions: Mail carriers spend most of their time outdoors and in all kinds of weather. They must lift heavy packages. Most start work very early in the morning.

Related Jobs: Mail clerk, messenger, merchandise deliverer, and delivery-route truckdriver

Subjects To Study Now and Later: Mathematics, English, geography, and physical education

Getting Ready and Places to Go to Observe: When mail arrives at your home, look at the letters and find the name, city, and state that it came from. Check the dates to see how long it took the letters to be delivered. Write and mail a letter to yourself. Call your local post office and ask if you can get a tour. Talk to your mail carrier about this job.

Tell Me More:

Local post offices and state employment service offices can supply details about entrance exams and job opportunities.

Mail Clerks

Education and Training:

A high school diploma is preferred.

Mail clerks sort and deliver internal mail in an organization.

Job Outlook:

Poor

Average Earnings:

Low

What They Do: Mail clerks help large businesses and governments run well by sorting and delivering mail, papers, and small packages to workers in the organization. Internal mail consists of reports or memos sent from one worker to another. Mail clerks also sort and deliver business mail from the U.S. Postal Service and mail going to the post office. Machines are sometimes used which fold and insert material into envelopes and put postage on the envelope.

Working Conditions: Mail clerks work in mailrooms, usually in office buildings. The mailrooms are sometimes noisy from sorting and folding machines. When not in the mailroom, the mail clerk is delivering mail throughout the office building.

Related Jobs: Postal clerk, mail carrier, route driver, traffic, shipping and receiving clerk, and parcel post clerk

Subjects To Study Now and Later: Mathematics, English, and typing

Getting Ready and Places to Go to Observe: Ask your parents if you can be in charge of the mail. Sort the day's mail into piles for every person in your home. Then deliver it. For all mail that leaves your home, you can place postage stamps on them. Sort the mail by putting the lowest zip code on top and the highest zip code on the bottom. Then, make sure it gets into a mailbox. Large office buildings have mailrooms. Call and ask a mailroom supervisor if you can visit to learn more about this career.

Tell Me More:

Mail Systems Management Association
J.A.F. Building
P.O. Box 2155
New York, NY 10116-2155

Order Clerks

 Education and Training:

A high school diploma is usually required. Some companies require technical knowledge about the products they sell.

 Job Outlook:

Good

Many order clerks deal mainly with the public.

 Average Earnings:

Low

What They Do: Order clerks handle orders that come into a business. Most of the orders are from customers. In large companies, some orders may be from one part of a company ordering parts from another part of the same company. Orders often come in by mail or fax machine. The order clerk reviews the order to make sure all necessary information is there. If an order is placed by telephone, the order clerk usually types the information into a computer system while on the telephone. Some order clerks adjust inventory records.

Working Conditions: Order clerks work indoors and sit a great deal. Many sit in front of a video display terminal.

Related Jobs: Bank teller, billing clerk, receiving clerk, hotel and motel clerk, credit clerk, file clerk, brokerage clerk, and medical record clerk

Subjects To Study Now and Later: Mathematics, English, typing, and business

Getting Ready and Places to Go to Observe: Work hard in school to get a good education. In high school, business classes will be helpful. Since order clerks often talk to people they have never met, it is important to be friendly and polite. Listen to how you speak with people. Are you friendly and polite to your friends and family? Mail order companies and other large businesses are good places to go to watch an order clerk. Ask your family or a neighbor if there are order clerks where they work.

 Tell Me More:

Association of Record Managers and Administrators (ARMA)
4200 Somerset Dr., Suite 215
Prairie Village, KS 66208

Payroll clerks record changes in employees' files.

 Education and Training:

A high school diploma is usually required.

 Job Outlook:

Good

 Average Earnings:

Low

What They Do: Payroll clerks make sure workers are paid correctly and on time. They review timecards to make sure they are correct. For example, they make sure the number of hours worked and sick or vacation days are correctly recorded. Payroll clerks figure how much pay the worker has earned. Then, the payroll clerk must subtract taxes or payments the worker puts towards various things like insurance and retirement. They often use computers. Some large companies have timekeeping clerks handle some of the timecard duties.

Working Conditions: Payroll clerks work indoors and sit a great deal. Payroll clerks may work at a video display terminal.

Related Jobs: Bank teller, billing clerk, receiving clerk, hotel and motel clerk, credit clerk, file clerk, brokerage clerk, and timekeeping clerk

Subjects To Study Now and Later: Mathematics, English, typing, and business

Getting Ready and Places to Go to Observe: Keep a record of how you spend your time. It is interesting to learn how much time we spend in school, sleeping, eating, or playing. How is the time you spend during the school week different than the time you are not in school? All businesses that have workers must have someone handle the payroll. Ask your family or a neighbor if there is someone who takes care of payroll that is willing to talk to you and tell you about their work.

 Tell Me More:

Association of Record Managers and Administrators (ARMA)
420 Somerset Dr., Suite 215
Prairie Village, KS 66208

Personnel Clerks

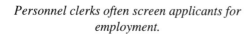
Personnel clerks often screen applicants for employment.

Education and Training:

A high school diploma is usually required.

Job Outlook:

Good

Average Earnings:

Low

What They Do: Personnel clerks greet new workers in a company. It is often the personnel clerk who will explain the company's benefits and rules to the new worker. Personnel clerks maintain the records of a company's workers, called personnel records. These records include information on workers, such as home address, pay increases, and evaluation reports. Personnel clerks also review applications and talk to people that are interested in working for the company.

Working Conditions: Personnel clerks work indoors and they sit a great deal. Personnel clerks may work at a video display terminal.

Related Jobs: Bank teller, billing clerk, receiving clerk, hotel and motel clerk, credit clerk, file clerk, brokerage clerk, and payroll clerk

Subjects To Study Now and Later: Mathematics, English, typing, and business

Getting Ready and Places to Go to Observe: In high school, business classes will be helpful. Since personnel clerks often must talk to people they have never met, it is important to be friendly and polite. Listen to how you speak with people. Are you friendly and polite to your friends and family? Large businesses hire personnel clerks. If you visit, ask them about what they do in their job and find out what they look for when they talk to people who are looking for a job.

Tell Me More:

Association of Record Managers and Administrators (ARMA)
420 Somerset Dr., Suite 215
Prairie Village, KS 66208

Receptionists help people when they first call or enter an office or building.

Education and Training:

A high school diploma is needed for this job. Community colleges and vocational schools offer classes.

Job Outlook:

Excellent

Average Earnings:

Low

What They Do: Receptionists greet people when they enter an office or call on the telephone. They also answer questions, give and get information, and take telephone messages. Computers are used to help with general office duties.

Working Conditions: Receptionists work inside in offices that are comfortable. They sit at a desk. This job requires working with people.

Related Jobs: Travel clerk, hotel desk clerk, airline reservation agent, and general office clerk

Subjects To Study Now and Later: Business, English, mathematics, and computer operations

Getting Ready and Places to Go to Observe: Be the family receptionist for one day. Answer the telephone and write down messages. Greet people that come to visit. If you have a computer, use it to help you write messages. Receptionists work in many local business offices like doctor's offices and insurance companies. Be on the lookout for other places where you will find receptionists at work.

Tell Me More:

The newspaper lists ads from companies that are hiring receptionists. The ads will give you information about job duties and wages.

Secretaries

Well qualified secretaries will continue to be in great demand.

 Education and Training:

A high school diploma and training in computer skills is needed for this job. Business schools and community colleges offer training programs.

 Job Outlook:

Excellent

 Average Earnings:

Medium

What They Do: Secretaries make appointments and travel arrangements. They answer the telephone, give information and receive visitors. They fill out forms, type letters and do filing.

Working Conditions: Secretaries work in places like offices, schools and hospitals. They sit most of the time and use computers. Some people work 40 hours each week, but others only work part-time.

Related Jobs: Bookkeeper, receptionist, personnel clerk, typist, legal assistant, and medical assistant

Subjects To Study Now and Later: Bookkeeping, computer operations, English, mathematics, and word processing

Getting Ready and Places to Go to Observe: Try being a secretary for a day at home. Answer the telephone and take messages. Get the mail, open it and give it to the right people. Write and send a letter to a friend or relative. Your school has a secretary. When you are in the school office watch the secretary at work. Many offices in your area have secretaries. Keep your eyes open for secretaries when you are at businesses.

 Tell Me More:

Professional Secretaries International
PO Box 20404
Kansas City, MO 64195-0404
http://www.gvi.net/psi

National Association of Legal Secretaries
2448 East 81st St., Suite 3400
Tulsa, OK 74137-4238
http://www.nals.org

Shipping and Receiving Clerks

Most shipping and receiving clerks work in urban areas.

Education and Training:

A high school diploma is needed for this job. Some companies have training programs.

Job Outlook:

Good

Average Earnings:

Low

What They Do: Shipping and receiving clerks receive goods, prepare shipments and keep records. Shipping clerks handle all goods being shipped out. Receiving clerks handle all goods that are delivered to the company. In small companies one person usually handles both duties. Large companies usually have several clerks. Computers are used by many clerks to help keep records.

Working Conditions: Shipping and receiving clerks work inside warehouses and outside on loading docks or both. This job requires standing, lifting and carrying. Most clerks work eight hours each day.

Related Jobs: Stock clerk, material clerk, distributing clerk, routing clerk, and express clerk

Subjects To Study Now and Later: English, mathematics, and computer operations

Getting Ready and Places to Go to Observe: Help your family prepare packages for shipping. On packages that you receive look at how they are packaged and labeled. Supermarkets have receiving departments. Ask if you can tour that department. Post offices have several clerks working in shipping and receiving.

Tell Me More:

National Retail Federation
325 7th St. NW, Suite 1000
Washington, DC 20004
http://www.nrf.com

Stenographers, Medical Transcriptionists, Court Reporters

Stenographers can advance to secretarial positions.

Depends on job.

Education and Training:

Stenographers learn their skills in high school, vocational school, or business school. Medical transcriptionists complete a vocational program. Court reporters complete a 2- or 4-year program after high school.

Depends on job.

Job Outlook:

Poor for stenographers; good for the other jobs.

Depends on job.

Average Earnings:

Low: Stenographers
Low - Medium: Medical Trans.
High: Court Reporters

What They Do: Stenographers provide reports of spoken words for correspondence, records, or legal proof. They take dictation by shorthand or use a stenotype machine. Some stenographers take dictation in foreign languages. Medical transcriptionists use a transcribing machine while listening to recordings by physicians and other healthcare professionals. They type and edit the recordings as necessary. Court reporters document all statements in an official judicial proceeding on a stenotype machine.

Working Conditions: Stenographers usually work in offices. Medical transcriptionists often work from home or in hospitals and doctors' offices. Court reporters usually work in the offices of attorneys, courtrooms.

Related Jobs: Bookkeeper, receptionist, secretary, medical assistant, and personnel clerk

Subjects To Study Now and Later: English, mathematics, shorthand, stenotype, computer operations, anatomy, and shorthand

Getting Ready and Places to Go to Observe: Practice, practice, practice on the computer to improve your skills and accuracy. Stenographers usually type 40 words per minute. These occupations can be found in many places including courts, hospitals, doctor's offices, and businesses in your area.

Tell Me More:

National Court Reporters Association
8224 Old Courthouse Rd.
Vienna, VA 22182
http://www.verbatimreporters.com

American Association for
  Medical Transcriptionists
P.O. Box 576187
Modesto, CA 95357
http://www.aamt.org/aamt

Education and Training:

High school diploma is preferred. Most people learn the duties while on the job.

Job Outlook:

Good

Average Earnings:

Low

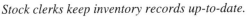
Stock clerks keep inventory records up-to-date.

What They Do: Stock clerks unpack products or delivered material. They make sure the correct items are in the cartons. They put the items in their proper place, organize them and keep records when they are removed. They may mark items with special codes. In stores, stock clerks may bring products to the sales area and put the products in their proper place on the shelf. In smaller companies, they do other duties such as filling orders.

Working Conditions: Stock clerks may work indoors in large warehouses or smaller stockrooms, depending on the type of business. They stand, bend, walk, lift, and carry a lot. They may work evenings and weekends.

Related Jobs: Shipping and receiving clerk, distributing clerk, routing clerk, stock supervisor, and cargo checker

Subjects To Study Now and Later: English, mathematics, physical education, and typing

Getting Ready and Places to Go to Observe: Organize a part of the kitchen. Notify a parent when you run out of an item that needs to be replaced. Many stores have stock clerks. Next time you are at the grocery store, shoe store or clothing store, see if you can find a stock clerk at work.

Tell Me More:

National Retail Federation
325 7th St., NW, Suite 1000
Washington, DC 20004
http://www.nrf.com

Teacher Aides

Teacher aides are also called paraprofessionals.

 Education and Training:

A high school diploma and sometimes college training is needed for this job. Many aides are trained on-the-job.

 Job Outlook:

Good

 Average Earnings:

Low

What They Do: Teacher aides assist classroom teachers. They help kids with learning, stock supplies, do filing, and grade tests and papers. They work with kids on projects and help supervise on field trips, at recess and in the classroom. Some teacher aides work with students in groups or individually.

Working Conditions: Teacher aides usually work part time during the school year. They work indoors in classrooms and outdoors on the playground. Their job requires standing, kneeling, and walking.

Related Jobs: Childcare worker, library technician, and library assistant

Subjects To Study Now and Later: English, mathematics, social studies, and computer operations

Getting Ready and Places to Go to Observe: Do you help your teacher with jobs? Do you have a teacher aide in your classroom? If you help pass out papers, clean and put away supplies, and help other students in your class, then you are doing some of the jobs that teacher aides also do. If you do not have a teacher aide ask if you can help.

 Tell Me More:

American Federation of Teachers, Organizing Department
555 New Jersey Ave. NW
Washington, DC 20001

National Resource Center for Paraprofessionals in Education and Related Services
25 West 43rd St., Room 620
New York, NY 10036

Telephone Operators

Employment of telephone operators is expected to decline.

 Education and Training:

Some employers require a high school diploma. Telephone companies often provide classroom and on-the-job training.

 Job Outlook:

Poor

 Average Earnings:

Low

What They Do: Telephone operators provide customer assistance with special needs like making collect calls, billing requests, and complaints. They also help people with other needs or emergencies. Some telephone operators work for answering service companies and businesses. Their main responsibility is answering the telephones, connecting the caller to the correct person, and taking messages.

Working Conditions: Telephone operators may work day, evening, or night shifts. They sometimes work weekends and holidays. Operators work indoors. They often sit at a video display terminal.

Related Jobs: Customer service representative, dispatcher, hotel clerk, receptionist, and travel clerk

Subjects To Study Now and Later: English, speech, mathematics, and computer operations

Getting Ready and Places to Go to Observe: Tape record your voice to see if you sound pleasant and polite. Good grades in reading, spelling, computer operations, and mathematics will be helpful in this job. Your local telephone company may provide a tour. Ask how many telephone operators work there and if you can watch them at work.

 Tell Me More:

United States Telephone
  Association
1401 A Street NW, Suite 600
Washington, DC 20005-2136

Communications Workers of America
Department of Apprenticeships,
  Benefits, and Employment
501 3rd St. NW
Washington, DC 20001

Word Processors & Data Entry Keyers

 Education and Training:

A high school diploma is usually necessary to begin work as a word processor or data entry keyer. Community colleges and business schools also have programs.

 Job Outlook:

Good

Word processors use equipment which includes a keyboard, video display terminal and a printer.

 Average Earnings:

Low

What They Do: Word processors use computers to enter large amounts of data, reports, letters, and mailing lists. They edit, store and revise information as needed. Some word processors handle work from several departments others may work in only one department. Data entry keyers usually fill forms that appear on a computer. Instead of a computer, data entry keyers may use a machine that is like a typewriter or they may use scanners to enter information.

Working Conditions: Word processors and data entry keyers usually work in offices. These jobs require sitting and doing the same motion for long periods of time. The office is sometimes loud from office machines.

Related Jobs: Stenographer, court reporter, telephone operator, and dispatcher

Subjects To Study Now and Later: English, mathematics, computer operations, and business courses

Getting Ready and Places to Go to Observe: Writing and working on a computer is the best way to begin learning about the work of word processors. Study the manuals that teach you the word processing system on your computer. Try to increase your speed by practicing keyboarding. Check with hospitals, banks and larger businesses in your area to see if they will let you tour their word processing department.

 Tell Me More:

Contact a State employment service office regarding job opportunities and information about data entry and word processing.

Service Occupations

This cluster includes jobs that usually require training in a two-year program. There will be many job openings due to high replacement needs from people leaving their jobs. A wide range of workers are covered in this cluster, including those from food preparation, health service, personal and cleaning services, and protective services. These jobs often have personal contact with people.

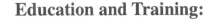

Chefs

Chefs often work evenings and weekends.

Education and Training:

Chefs have experience or attend two to four year training programs at vocational schools, colleges or culinary institutes. Some hotels and restaurants have training programs.

Job Outlook:

Excellent

Average Earnings:

Low - Medium

What They Do: Chefs prepare meals that taste and look good. They have more industrial training and skills than cooks. Institutional chefs work in hospitals, schools, and cafeterias. They prepare one meal in mass quantities each day. Restaurant chefs fix several dishes and cook each serving separately for the person ordering. Chefs use recipes to prepare food and sometimes help plan meals and new dishes.

Working Conditions: Chefs work in kitchens that can be modern and air-conditioned or small and not as up-to-date. They stand for long periods of time. Some heavy lifting is required.

Related Jobs: Butcher, meatcutter, cannery worker, and industrial baker

Subjects To Study Now and Later: English, mathematics, chemistry, health, and home economics

Getting Ready and Places to Go to Observe: Helping to plan, prepare and serve healthy meals to your family is a good way to see if you like doing the work of a chef. Try different meals and ideas. The food needs to look and taste good. Your school and local restaurants have chefs. Visit them both to see the difference in their jobs and schedules.

Tell Me More:

The National Restaurant Association
1200 17th St. NW
Washington, DC 20036-3097

American Culinary Federation
P.O. Box 3466
St. Augustine, FL 32085

Food Service Workers

Waiters and waitresses are on their feet most of the time.

 Education and Training:

Many teenagers have food service jobs while finishing high school. Most workers learn on-the-job.

 Job Outlook:

Excellent

 Average Earnings:

Low

What They Do: Food service workers take customers' orders, serve food and drinks, and prepare the check. They work many places including small coffee shops or large fine restaurants. Other duties may include seating customers, taking payments, and clearing tables.

Working Conditions: Food service workers are on their feet for long periods of time. This job requires lifting heavy trays of food. Many food service workers work evenings, weekends, and holidays. Most jobs are part-time.

Related Jobs: Flight attendant, butler, and tour busdriver

Subjects To Study Now and Later: English, mathematics, home economics, and speech

Getting Ready and Places to Go to Observe: Helping your family with meals will give you an idea of the jobs done by food service workers. Help prepare, serve, and clean up. When you are in different kinds of restaurants watch the food service workers at work. Ask them what they like about their job.

 Tell Me More:

National Restaurant Association
1200 South Wacker Dr., Suite 1400
Washington, DC 20036-3097

Council on Hotel, Restaurant, and
  Institutional Education
1200 17th St. NW
Washington, DC 20036-3097

Dental Assistants

 Education and Training:

Attending a one- to two-year training program is usually required. Some learn on-the-job.

Job Outlook:

Excellent

One out of three dental assistants work part-time.

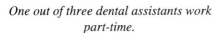

Average Earnings:

Low

What They Do: Dental assistants have many job duties. They get patients' dental records, prepare patients for treatment, and assist the dentist at chairside when treating patients. Other jobs include sterilizing equipment, restocking supplies, and teaching patients about oral health care. Some dental assistants also do office or laboratory job duties.

Working Conditions: Dental assistants wear gloves and masks to protect themselves from disease and germs.

Related Jobs: Medical assistant, physical therapy assistant, occupational therapy assistant, and pharmacy technician and assistant

Subjects To Study Now and Later: English, mathematics, health, biology, chemistry, and bookkeeping

Getting Ready and Places to Go to Observe: Learn how to take good care of teeth and gums. When you go to the dentist, watch the dental assistant. Ask questions about the different tools that are used.

 Tell Me More:

Dental Assisting National Board, Inc.
216 E. Ontario St.
Chicago, IL 60611

Commission on Dental Accreditation
American Dental Association
211 E. Chicago Ave., Suite 1814
Chicago, IL 60611
http://www.ada.org

Medical Assistants

Demand for medical assistants will grow much faster than most jobs.

 Education and Training:

A high school diploma is usually required. Some medical assistants are trained on-the-job. Training is available at some schools and colleges.

 Job Outlook:

Excellent

 Average Earnings:

Low

What They Do: Medical assistants' duties include helping the physician with patients and doing some office jobs. They take medical histories, do lab tests, take care of supplies, prepare people for X-rays, call in prescriptions, and draw blood. Office jobs include answering the telephone, filling out insurance forms, and making patient appointments.

Working Conditions: Medical assistants work in offices. This job requires working with people. Sometimes evening and weekend work is needed.

Related Jobs: Medical secretary, hospital admitting clerk, medical records clerk, dental assistant, and occupational therapy aid

Subjects To Study Now and Later: Mathematics, health, biology, bookkeeping, and computer operations

Getting Ready and Places to Go to Observe: If you like helping people, working on the computer, and keeping things orderly you have some of the interests of a medical assistant. With books from the library, learn about health and medical work. Local physicians have medical assistants that work in their offices.

 Tell Me More:

The American Association of
    Medical Assistants
20 North Wacker Dr., Suite 1575
Chicago, IL 60606-2903

Registered Medical Assistants of
    American Medical Technologists
710 Higgins Rd.
Park Ridge, IL 60068-5765

Many nursing aides gain satisfaction from assisting those in need.

Education and Training:

While a high school diploma is not required, some companies require training or experience. Vocational-technical schools and community colleges provide training.

Job Outlook:

Excellent

Average Earnings:

Low

What They Do: Nursing aides help care for physically ill, injured, or disabled people. These people are usually in hospitals or nursing homes. Nursing aides work under the supervision of nursing and medical staff. They serve meals, make beds, feed, dress and bathe patients. They may also take temperatures and blood pressures. In nursing homes, they are often the main person who cares for the patient. Since these patients are sometimes in a nursing home for a long time, nursing aides often develop close relationships with them.

Working Conditions: Nursing aides work indoors. Some work evenings, weekends, and holidays. Many hours are spent standing or helping patients walk and get in and out of bed.

Related Jobs: Psychiatric aide, homemaker-home health aide, childcare worker, companion, occupational therapy aide, and physical therapy aide

Subjects To Study Now and Later: Biology, anatomy and physiology, psychology, sociology, and English

Getting Ready and Places to Go to Observe: This career requires patience, understanding, and a desire to help people. Think about what you say to people. Can you be more patient with a sister or brother? Do you help your parents before they ask? Are you understanding with your friends when they make mistakes? Visit a nursing home and ask if a nursing aide has a few minutes to spend with you to explain about the job and why they enjoy it.

Tell Me More:

National Association of Health Career Schools
750 First St. NE Suite 940
Washington, DC 20002
Email: *NAHCS@aol.com*

Occupational Therapy Assistants & Aides

 Education and Training:

An assistant needs an associate's degree or certificate from an accredited college. An aide must have a high school diploma.

 Job Outlook:

Good

Occupational therapy assistants and aides improve quality of life by helping patients overcome limitations.

 Average Earnings:

Low - Medium

What They Do: Occupational therapy assistants and aides work for occupational therapists. They work with persons who have mental, physical or emotional impairments. Occupational therapist assistants help clients improve their quality of life with activities and exercises developed with the occupational therapist. These activities can range from teaching someone how to stretch without causing further injury to moving from a bed into a wheelchair. An occupational therapist aide may also prepare materials and put together the equipment used during a therapy session.

Working Conditions: Occupational therapy assistants and aides work indoors. They are on their feet a lot and may need to help lifting and moving patients or equipment.

Related Jobs: Occupational therapist, dental assistant, medical assistant, optometric assistant, pharmacy assistant and physical therapy assistant and aide

Subjects To Study Now and Later: Psychology, anatomy, physiology, biology, health, and English

Getting Ready and Places to Go to Observe: Contact a local hospital, nursing care facility or occupational therapy clinic. Find out if you can observe an assistant at work.

 Tell Me More:

For information on a career as an occupational therapy assistant or a list of accredited programs, send a self-addressed label and $5.00 to:

The American Occupational
 Therapy Association
4720 Montgomery Lane
Bethesda, MD 20824-1220
http://www.aota.org

Physical Therapy Assistants & Aides

Physical therapy assistants and aides receive on-the-job training.

Education and Training:

An aide is required to have a high school diploma. An assistant needs an associate's degree.

Job Outlook:

Excellent

Average Earnings:

Low - Medium

What They Do: Physical therapy assistants and aides assist physical therapists. Their patients are physically disabled due to accidents or other health reasons, such as arthritis and heart disease. Physical therapy assistants perform many tasks, such as giving massages and assisting with ultrasound. Physical therapy aides help the physical therapist by preparing for each patient's therapy and keeping the treatment area clean and organized. They may push patients in a wheelchair. Both assistants and aides perform clerical tasks, such as maintaining patient records and filling out insurance forms.

Working Conditions: Physical therapy assistants and aides need to have strength in order to help patients with their treatment. They may work evening and weekend hours.

Related Jobs: Dental assistant, medical assistant, occupational therapy assistant, optometric assistant, recreational therapy assistant, and pharmacy assistant

Subjects To Study Now and Later: Mathematics, health, biology, chemistry, psychology, CPR, and first aid

Getting Ready and Places to Go to Observe: Call ahead and find out if you can visit a rehabilitation center in your area. Most hospitals have outpatient services and there are many clinics around the country. In sports physical therapy, physical therapist assistants help on the sidelines at sporting events.

Tell Me More:

The American Physical Therapy Association
111 North Fairfax St.
Alexandria, VA 22314-1488

http://www.apta.org

Animal Caretakers

Animal caretakers feed animals and clean them.

 Education and Training:

There are no formal education requirements needed to become an animal caretaker. Many people are trained on-the-job. Employers look for people that have experience in working with animals.

 Job Outlook:

Excellent

 Average Earnings:

Low

What They Do: Animal caretakers attend to the daily needs of animals. They feed, bathe, groom and exercise them. They keep the animals cages clean and make sure there is plenty of food and water. Animal caretakers play with animals and watch for signs of injury or illness.

Working Conditions: Animals caretakers work indoors and outdoors. This job requires lifting and is sometimes noisy. Animals need 24 hour care, so some caretakers work weekends, evenings, and holidays.

Related Jobs: Animal breeder, animal trainer, livestock farm worker, veterinarian, wildlife biologist, and zookeeper

Subjects To Study Now and Later: English, mathematics, science, and animal care and management

Getting Ready and Places to Go to Observe: Offer to take care of a neighbor's animal while they are away, or keep a school pet that needs care over vacation. Learn about different animals which are often kept as pets. Zoos, animal shelters, pet stores, and veterinary clinics all hire animal caretakers.

 Tell Me More:

The Humane Society of the
   United States
2100 L Street. NW
Washington, DC 20037-1598

American Boarding Kennel
   Association
4575 Galley Rd., Suite 400-A
Colorado Springs, CO 80915
http://www.abka.com

Cosmetologists

Cosmetologists must know about the newest hairstyles.

 Education and Training:

Some states require a high school degree. A six-month to two-year training program is usually required.

 Job Outlook:

Good

 Average Earnings:

Low - Medium

What They Do: Cosmetologists cut, trim, shampoo and style hair to help people look their best. They advise customers on how to care for their hair, skin and makeup. Cosmetologists lighten, darken, or completely change the color of hair. They often straighten or give waves. Men also have their beards and moustaches trimmed by a cosmetologist.

Working Conditions: Cosmetologists work indoors, standing most of the time. Evenings and weekends must often be worked.

Related Jobs: Beauty consultant, beauty supply distributor and salon manager

Subjects To Study Now and Later: Mathematics, English, health sciences and art

Getting Ready and Places to Go to Observe: Practice styling your own hair. Older teenagers can practice on family members. If someone you know has a wig or hairpiece that they don't want anymore, you can style it in different ways. Look at magazines and notice the style of hair on models. The best place to see a cosmetologist at work is in a hair styling shop, called a beauty salon. You may already go to one to get your hair cut.

 Tell Me More:

National Cosmetology
    Association, Inc.
3510 Olive St.
St. Louis, MO 63017

National Accrediting Commission of
    Cosmetology Arts and Sciences
901 North Stuart St., Suite 900
Arlington, VA 22203-1816

Flight Attendants

Education and Training:

Flight attendants need a high school diploma. College or experience is preferred. Training is provided by the airline after hiring.

Job Outlook:

Good

Flight attendants have the opportunity to travel and see new places.

Average Earnings:

Low - Medium

What They Do: Flight attendants assist people traveling on passenger planes. Before the flight they check supplies and equipment, and discuss flight information with the captain. They collect passenger tickets, help find seats, and store carry-on items. Flight attendants serve food and drinks on some flights. They operate emergency equipment if necessary and give first aid.

Working Conditions: Flight attendants work different hours and sometimes weekends, evenings, and holidays. Staying away from home is often necessary, but hotel and food expenses are paid by the airline.

Related Jobs: Gate agent, tour guide, camp counselor, and waiter/waitress

Subjects To Study Now and Later: English, mathematics, first aid, physical education, and foreign languages

Getting Ready and Places to Go to Observe: If you fly on a passenger plane keep a watchful eye on all the duties that flight attendants perform. At home you can try assisting your family for two hours before, during, and after dinner. Seat them, serve them, clean up the table, and take care of all their needs. Airports have flight attendants going to and from work. Call an airline and ask if they have a flight attendant that you can talk to about the job.

Tell Me More:

Write to the personnel manager of an airline for further information on being a light attendant. See the beginning of this book for an example of one way to write a letter.

Job openings for gardeners should be plentiful.

 ### Education and Training:

Many gardeners have experience by working in a nursery or at home. A good driving record and getting along with people is needed. Some states require a certificate to work with chemicals.

 ### Job Outlook:

Excellent

 ### Average Earnings:

Low

What They Do: Gardeners take care of lawns, gardens, trees, flowers, and shrubs. They work on large and small areas, like around office buildings or private homes. They mow lawns, water, prune trees, shrubs, and plants. Sometimes gardeners follow landscape plans and plant entire areas.

Working Conditions: Gardeners work with tools and machinery. They work outdoors in all kinds of weather. There may be more work during the spring and summer months. This job requires working with some chemicals.

Related Jobs: Construction worker, horticultural worker, farmer, landscape architect, tree surgeon helpers, and soil conservation technicians

Subjects To Study Now and Later: English, mathematics, biology, horticulture, and botany

Getting Ready and Places to Go to Observe: Plant a garden, help out in your own yard, or find an indoor plant and take care of it. Volunteer to care for a neighbor's yard and garden when they are out of town. Books from the library will guide you about what kind of care is needed for different months of the year. Check with your local nursery for gardeners that work in your area. Ask your family or neighbors about the way they care for their yards.

 Tell Me More:

Associated Landscape Contractors
   of America, Inc.
12200 Sunrise Valley Dr., Suite 150
Reston, VA 20191

Professional Grounds
   Management Society
120 Cockeysville Rd., Suite 104
Hunt Valley, MD 21031

Homemaker-Home Health Aides

Homemaker-home health aides generally work with little supervision.

 Education and Training:

The Federal Government requires passing a test and completing 75 hours of training.

 Job Outlook:

Excellent

 Average Earnings:

Low

What They Do: Homemaker-home health aides help elderly, disabled, and ill persons live in their own homes instead of in a nursing home. Some work in homes where there are small children who also need care. These aides do housekeeping, such as cleaning the home and cooking. They do personal care, like assisting with bathing and hair care. Another important part of their job is to listen to people talk about their problems.

Working Conditions: Homemaker-home health aides work indoors caring for people. Sometimes they spend many days, weeks or months in one home. Other times, they may visit many homes in one day.

Related Jobs: Childcare attendant, nursing aide, companion, nursery school attendant, physical therapy aide, psychiatric aide and occupational therapy aide

Subjects To Study Now and Later: First aid, health sciences, mathematics, home economics, nutrition, and English

Getting Ready and Places to Go to Observe: Homemaker-home health aides must be cheerful and like to help people. They also must be honest and good listeners. These are all good qualities that you can continue to develop. Go to your library to learn about good health habits. Ask your doctor if there is a homemaker-home health aide who may be willing to talk to you. Relatives or neighbors may also know of someone who is an aide.

 Tell Me More:

National Association for Home Care
228 7th St. SE
Washington, DC 20003

National Association of Health
  Career Schools
750 First St. NE, Suite 940
Washington, DC 20002

Some janitors work in schools.

Education and Training:
Most janitors learn on the job.

Job Outlook:
Good

Average Earnings:
Low

What They Do: Janitors clean and maintain offices, hospitals, stores and many other places of business. Some also do repair work. Janitors need to be able to follow directions. They need to know the correct way to use equipment and supplies when cleaning. Some janitors work for one company, but many janitors work for more than one business.

Working Conditions: This job sometimes requires evening and weekend work when businesses are closed. Some outdoor work may be needed but most work is done indoors. Janitors stand most of the time. Heavy lifting is sometimes necessary.

Related Jobs: Refuse collector, floor waxer, street sweeper, window cleaner, and gardener

Subjects To Study Now and Later: Shop, industrial arts, and English

Getting Ready and Places to Go to Observe: Help in your classroom or home doing the jobs that janitors perform. Empty the trash, vacuum, wash floors, and clean bathrooms. Your school has one or more janitors that work daily cleaning and taking care of repairs. Ask them questions about the equipment they use and the job duties that they do.

Tell Me More:
Instructional Executive Housekeepers Association, Inc.
1001 Eastwind Dr., Suite 301
Westerville, OH 43081-3361
http://www.ieha.org

Preschool Workers

 Education and Training:

Requirements vary between states. They range from a high school diploma to a college degree. Some states require passing a test and completing special training classes.

 Job Outlook:

Excellent

 Average Earnings:

Low

One of the rewards of a preschool worker is watching children grow and gain new skills.

What They Do: Preschool workers teach and care for children who are younger than five years old. Preschool workers may work in large daycare centers or in family daycare homes. They keep records of a child's physical and emotional development. They discuss individual needs of the child with the parents. Preschool workers are important to the health and development of the children they teach.

Working Conditions: Preschool workers are indoors and outdoors with children. They stand, walk, bend, and lift a lot. Work hours vary and can range from early morning to late evening, depending on the needs of the parents.

Related Jobs: Teacher aide, children's tutor, kindergarten and elementary school teacher, and early childhood program director

Subjects To Study Now and Later: Home economics, psychology, sociology, and English

Getting Ready and Places to Go to Observe: Being around young children is the best way to learn how to work with them. Many teenagers babysit and learn how well they work with children. There are babysitting courses available in some communities which teach first aid as well as how to care for young children. There is usually a daycare center in every community. Visit a local daycare center and ask if you can observe. Ask the teachers if you can talk to them when they are on a break. What do they like and dislike about their job?

 Tell Me More:

National Association for the
   Education of Young Children
1509 16th St. NW
Washington, DC 20036

Association for Childhood
   Education International
11501 Georgia Ave., #315
Wheaton, MD 20902-1924

Private Household Workers

Private household workers have a variety of duties.

 Education and Training:

There is no required education for this career. Most jobs require the skill to clean well, cook, or take care of children. There are schools that provide training.

 Job Outlook:

Excellent

 Average Earnings:

Low

What They Do: Private household workers work in the homes of people who hire them. They may care for infants or children, clean homes, or plan and cook meals. Others care for people who are elderly, handicapped or recovering from an illness or accident. There are private household workers who are responsible for running an entire home. They answer telephones and serve meals. Private household workers may work for only one household or they may work for many.

Working Conditions: Private household workers usually work in nice and comfortable homes or apartments. Some live in their own homes. Others live in the home of their employer. There may be a lot of standing, lifting, walking, bending and reaching.

Related Jobs: Building custodian, hotel and restaurant cleaner, childcare worker, home health aide, and cook

Subjects To Study Now and Later: English, first aid, business, and home economics

Getting Ready and Places to Go to Observe: Help plan a dinner. Learn how to make a grocery shopping list using the amount of money you have available to spend. Help your parents watch younger brothers or sisters. Find out about classes, for young people, that provide training for babysitting. Visit a daycare center. When you go to restaurants, watch the waitpersons. Ask your parents if they know anyone who has a private household worker working in their home. If they do, find out if you can meet with them and ask them questions.

 Tell Me More:

American Council of Nanny Schools
Delta College
University Center, MI 48710

Correction Officers

Correction officers monitor the activities of prisoners.

Education and Training:

Correction officers need to have a high school diploma and be a United States citizen. There are health requirements in some states. College education is preferred. Training can take up to a few months.

Job Outlook:

Excellent

Average Earnings:

Low - Medium

What They Do: Correction officers work in prisons. They are in charge of the security and safety of people who have been arrested, are serving prison sentences or are waiting to go to trial. They counsel, enforce rules and supervise all activities. They inspect living quarters and mail for security reasons. Correction officers keep track of inmates at all times.

Working Conditions: Correction officers work indoors and outdoors. Some prisons are loud, hot, and overcrowded. Security is needed 24-hours each day so some work is required on weekends and holidays. The work can be dangerous.

Related Jobs: Probation and parole officers, bodyguard, detective, security guard, and police officer

Subjects To Study Now and Later: English, physical education, and mathematics

Getting Ready and Places to Go to Observe: Being physically fit is important. If you like helping your community and working with others you have some interests that correction officers need. The correctional institution in your area may have tours that let you see correctional officers at work.

Tell Me More:

Federal Bureau of Prisons
Office of Personnel Management
http://www.usa.jobs.opm.gov

Firefighters

Fire departments are also responsible for fire prevention.

 Education and Training:

A high school diploma is required. They must pass a written and physical fitness test. Experience as a volunteer, high test scores, and training or schooling is helpful. Some colleges offer degrees.

 Job Outlook:

Poor

 Average Earnings:

Low - Medium

What They Do: Firefighters battle fires and other related emergencies. They work as a team and follow the directions of a superior. Duties include connecting hoses, moving ladders, and rescuing victims. They also work in areas of fire prevention by inspecting buildings and speaking at civic groups and schools. Firefighters also write reports and continue physical training when not fighting fires.

Working Conditions: Firefighting is a job that can be dangerous. Firefighters sometimes work shifts of 24 hours, including weekends and holidays.

Related Jobs: Fire-protection engineer, police officer, and emergency medical technician

Subjects To Study Now and Later: Physical education, English, mathematics, and chemistry

Getting Ready and Places to Go to Observe: Fire prevention is very important. Draw an emergency escape plan for your home with two ways to exit from each room. Check your home smoke alarms to be sure they are working correctly. In case of a fire where will your family meet away from the home? Ask your parents if you can have a family fire drill. Talk to firefighters in your area about fire safety. Ask for a tour of the fire station in your area. Talk to the firefighters on duty about their job.

 Tell Me More:

U.S. Fire Administration
16825 South Seton Ave.
Emmitsburg, MD 21727

International Association of
  Fire Fighters
1750 New York Ave. NW
Washington, DC 20006

Guards

Guards provide protection against theft.

 Education and Training:

Most guards need a high school diploma. Guards must usually be at least 18 years old with no criminal record, and complete a training program.

 Job Outlook:

Excellent

 Average Earnings:

Low

What They Do: Guards protect people, property, and things. They have different duties in different jobs. Guards keep watch over buildings, stores, and banks. At airports they check passengers for weapons and other illegal items. Some guards work at sporting events and conferences to help with crowd control. They wear uniforms and sometimes carry guns or other weapons.

Working Conditions: Guards work indoors and outdoors. They work at a guard desk and sometimes patrol areas on foot. Guards work various hours, including weekends and evenings. The night shift usually works alone with radio contact to a head office.

Related Jobs: Bailiff, detective, correction officer, and private investigator

Subjects To Study Now and Later: Physical education, English, mathematics, and computer operations

Getting Ready and Places to Go to Observe: Review how secure your home is with your parents. Make a list of the things that need to be checked each night before going to bed. Check to be sure doors are locked and windows shut. Banks, hospitals, and large businesses sometimes have guards at work. Keep your eyes open as you go to different businesses to see guards working.

 Tell Me More:

Check the telephone directory listings under security for an address to write to for more information about this job.

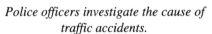

Police officers investigate the cause of traffic accidents.

Education and Training:

A high school diploma and one to four years of college is usually required. To apply for a police officer, usually one must be at least 20 years old and be physically fit.

Job Outlook:

Poor

Average Earnings:

Medium

What They Do: Police officers are responsible for the safety and security of people and property. Their duties may range from controlling traffic or giving first aid to an accident victim, to preventing and solving crimes. Some police officers specialize in areas such as handwriting and fingerprint identification. Police officers who work in small communities have a wider range of duties than those working in large cities.

Working Conditions: Police officers work indoors part of the time. Some may work outdoors for long periods in all kinds of weather. Nights, weekends, and holidays may need to be worked. Police work can be very dangerous.

Related Jobs: State police officer, detective, FBI special agent, guard, correction officer, deputy sheriff, fire marshal, and U.S. marshal

Subjects To Study Now and Later: Physical education, English, mathematics, sociology and psychology

Getting Ready and Places to Go to Observe: Keeping yourself in good physical condition is important. Be active and eat well. Attend Red Cross first aid classes. There are books you can read if you are interested. Police departments work hard to reach the people in their community. Many offer tours of their buildings.

Tell Me More:

U.S. Secret Service
Personnel Division, Room 912
1800 G St. NW
Washington, DC 20223

United States Marshals Service
Employment and Compensation Div.
Field Staffing Branch
600 Army Navy Dr.
Arlington, VA 22202

Mechanics, Installers and Repairers Occupations

The workers in this cluster adjust, maintain, and repair different types of equipment, including automobiles and computers. They work with tools. Many of their skills are learned on-the-job or in community and vocational colleges.

Aircraft Mechanics

  Education and Training:

Additional training of two to three years is required after high school. Some learn their job in the armed forces. Many mechanics must be FAA certified to work on civilian aircraft.

 Job Outlook:

Excellent

Aircraft mechanics must follow established procedures to meet Federal inspection standards.

 Average Earnings:

Medium

What They Do: Aircraft mechanics check engines, landing gear and other parts of aircraft for worn or defective parts. They replace or repair the problem and test it. Some aircraft mechanics work on several different types of aircraft, others may work on only one type of aircraft. Special tools, like X-rays, are used to check for invisible cracks and other defects. They have a lot of responsibility to make sure the aircraft is safe to fly.

Working Conditions: Aircraft mechanics work indoors and outdoors at airports. They must be able to lift heavy parts. There is a lot of noise from engines.

Related Jobs: Electrician, elevator repairer, and telephone maintenance mechanic

Subjects To Study Now and Later: Mathematics, physics, chemistry, English, electronics, computer science, and mechanical drawing

Getting Ready and Places to Go to Observe: Books from the library can help you learn more about aviation and how airplanes fly. Airports have many aircraft mechanics on duty. Contact an airport nearby to see if you can have a tour.

 Tell Me More:

Future Aviation Professionals
    of America
4959 Massachusetts Blvd.
Atlanta, GA 30338

Professional Aviation
    Maintenance Association
1200 18th St. NW, Suite 401
Washington, DC 20036

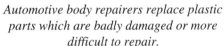

Automotive body repairers replace plastic parts which are badly damaged or more difficult to repair.

Education and Training:

A high school diploma is preferred. Training programs are offered at high schools, community colleges and vocational schools. On-the-job training takes four to five years.

Job Outlook:

Good

Average Earnings:

Medium

What They Do: Automotive body repairers fix damaged cars, trucks, and other motor vehicles. By using special machines and tools, they fix dents, replace parts, remove damaged sections, and straighten frames. Some automotive body repairers also paint the vehicles after repairing them.

Working Conditions: Automotive body repairers work in body shops that have a high level of noise. Shops need to be well ventilated because of dust and paint fumes.

Related Jobs: Auto mechanic, aircraft mechanic, painter, and electronic equipment repairer

Subjects To Study Now and Later: English, mathematics, shop, drafting, blueprint reading, and welding

Getting Ready and Places to Go to Observe: Have you ever put together a model of a miniature car or truck? Models show many of the different parts that automotive body repairers fix or replace. Cars are made of different types of materials. Watch other cars on the road. Can you tell from what materials they are made? Most automotive body repairers work in body shops. Look in your telephone directory for body shops in your area.

Tell Me More:

Automotive Service
  Association, Inc.
1901 Airport Freeway
Bedford, TX 76021-5732

Automotive Service Industry
  Association
25 Northwest Point
Elk Grove Village, IL 60007-1035

Automotive Mechanics

An automotive mechanic must be able to diagnose the source of a problem quickly and accurately.

 Education and Training:

After high school, a six-month to two-year formal training program is recommended.

 Job Outlook:

Good

 Average Earnings:

Medium - High

What They Do: Automotive mechanics repair and service cars, trucks, vans, and pickups. First they must find out what the problem is and then know how to repair or replace it. They also do regular maintenance work to keep the vehicle running properly. Some automotive mechanics specialize in one area of repair like air conditioning. Other mechanics work in all areas of automotive repair.

Working Conditions: Most automotive mechanics work indoors in repair shops. The shop may be loud and parts are dirty and greasy.

Related Jobs: Diesel truck and bus mechanic, motorcycle mechanic, and automotive body repairer

Subjects To Study Now and Later: English, mathematics, mechanics, drafting, and physics

Getting Ready and Places to Go to Observe: Watch someone with experience doing repair work on a car. Ask about the parts of a car. What needs to be done to maintain a car regularly, like changing the oil? Car dealerships often have mechanics on duty. Ask if you can tour the shop and talk to an automotive mechanic.

 Tell Me More:

National Automotive Technicians Education Foundation 13505 Dulles Technology Dr. Herndon, VA 22071-3415

Automotive Service Association 1901 Airport Freeway Bedford, TX 76021-5732

Electronic Equipment Repairers

 Education and Training:

One to two years of formal training after high school is required.

 Job Outlook:

Poor

Average Earnings:

Medium

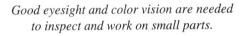
Good eyesight and color vision are needed to inspect and work on small parts.

What They Do: Electronic equipment repairers take care of electronic equipment used in many places including businesses, factories, hospitals, and homes. They install and repair televisions, computers, telephone systems, medical equipment, and many other types of electronic equipment. Detailed records are kept on the service they perform. They diagnose and repair problems, often using small hand tools such as pliers and soldering guns.

Working Conditions: Electronic equipment repairers work indoors or outdoors depending on the type of repair. Some jobs require working outside on rooftops or telephone poles. This job requires heavy lifting, crawling, and climbing on rooftops.

Related Jobs: Appliance and powertool repairer, automotive electrician, vending machine repairer, and broadcast technician

Subjects To Study Now and Later: Mathematics, physics, electronics, computer operations, and English

Getting Ready and Places to Go to Observe: Learn as much as you can about repairing electronic equipment by getting books from the library. Ask if you can observe when a repairer comes to your home or school to repair a computer or television. With adult supervision, take apart an old radio that does not work anymore. Visit a retail store that sells equipment like televisions or computers. Ask them if they have an electronic equipment repairer working there that you can talk to about the job.

 Tell Me More:

The International Society of Certified
　Electronics Technicians
2708 West Berry St.
Fort Worth, TX 76109

Electronics Technicians Association
602 North Jackson
Greencastle, IN 46135

Computer Repairers

Computer repairers run diagnostic programs to find problems.

Education and Training:

Computer repairers need one to two years of training after high school

Job Outlook:

Excellent

Average Earnings:

Medium

What They Do: Computer repairers work on all types of computer. They diagnose problems, install, repair, and maintain equipment. It is necessary to know about hardware and software in order to be able to run special software programs that help find problems. When installing equipment, they must work closely with electricians.

Working Conditions: Computer repairers work indoors for many different businesses. They may work evenings, weekends, and holidays.

Related Jobs: Appliance and powertool repairer, automotive electrician, vending machine repairer, and office machine repairer

Subjects To Study Now and Later: English, mathematics, physics, computer operations, and drafting

Getting Ready and Places to Go to Observe: Study and learn as much as you can about computers. If you know people that work with computers ask questions about how to set up and install new computers. Find out who repairs their computer. Some large computer companies have repairers that work for them in all states. Look in your local yellow pages for a computer repairer near you.

Tell Me More:

The International Society of Certified
  Electronics Technicians
2708 West Berry St.
Fort Worth, TX 76109

General Maintenance Mechanics

General maintenance mechanics often do a variety of tasks.

 Education and Training:

A high school and vocational school education is preferred. Most general maintenance mechanics learn their skills on-the-job.

 Job Outlook:

Excellent

 Average Earnings:

Low

What They Do: General maintenance mechanics do a wide variety of maintenance and repair work. They work on machines and buildings. They repair plumbing, electrical, air-conditioning and heating systems. Typical duties also might include painting, fixing roofs, and unclogging drains. General maintenance mechanics are often called "jacks-of-all-trades" because they work in so many areas of construction trades.

Working Conditions: General maintenance mechanics work outdoors and indoors, depending on the work that needs to be done. They may stand for long periods, lift heavy objects, and work in very hot or cold areas. They sometimes work nights or weekends.

Related Jobs: Carpenter, plumber, industrial machinery mechanic, electrician, and air-conditioning, refrigeration and heating mechanic

Subjects To Study Now and Later: Mechanical drawing, electricity, woodworking, blueprint reading, science, mathematics, and English

Getting Ready and Places to Go to Observe: Ask an adult who does repair work if you can watch. Have the steps involved explained to you. There are good books at your library you can read which explain how mechanical things work. When repair and maintenance work is being done at your home, ask the repairer if you can watch.

 Tell Me More:

National Association of Trade & Technical Schools
P.O. Box 20006
Annapolis Junction, MD 20701-2006

Heating & Air Conditioning Technicians

Heating and air-conditioning technicians follow blueprints and manufacturers' instructions.

 Education and Training:

One to two years of formal training after high school is preferred.

 Job Outlook:

Excellent

 Average Earnings:

Low - Medium

What They Do: Heating and air conditioning technicians install heating and air conditioning systems and units. They use ducts, pumps, fans, and many other parts. They also service or repair systems as needed. They use special tools including voltmeters and thermometers to help them diagnose and fix problems.

Working Conditions: Heating and air conditioning technicians work both indoors and outdoors. They sometimes work in high places, and stand or kneel a lot. Some evening and weekend work is needed.

Related Jobs: Boilermaker, electrical appliance servicer, electrician, and plumber

Subjects To Study Now and Later: English, mathematics, electronics, welding, metalworking, physics, and drafting

Getting Ready and Places to Go to Observe: Most businesses and homes in your area have heating and sometimes air conditioning systems. Check your phone directory for a local list of heating and air conditioning technicians. Ask them what they like and dislike about their work.

 Tell Me More:

Associated Builders and Contractors
1300 N. 17th St.
Rosslyn, VA 22209

National Association of Plumbing-
Heating-Cooling Contractors
PO Box 6808
Falls Church, VA 22046

Line Installers

Line installers usually work in all kinds of weather and are subject to 24-hour calls.

 Education and Training:

A high school diploma is preferred. Many companies test people's skills before they hire them.

 Job Outlook:

Poor

 Average Earnings:

Medium

What They Do: Line installers lay the wires and cables which allow you to watch television, use electricity and talk on the telephone. They install poles and equipment to hang these wires and cables, which are also called lines. They climb poles or use trucks that raise them to where the wires and cables are attached. Line installers also lay cable underground. Some line installers also maintain and repair the wires and cables.

Working Conditions: Line installers work outdoors in all kinds of weather. They must do a lot of climbing, lifting, and bending. They may have to work at all hours of the day and night.

Related Jobs: Communications equipment mechanic, biomedical equipment technician, sound technician, telephone installer and repairer, and electrician

Subjects To Study Now and Later: Mathematics, physical education, English, mechanics, and shop

Getting Ready and Places to Go to Observe: Contact your telephone company. They may have additional information on how you can learn more about the work of line installers. You can sometimes see line installers working in your neighborhood. Watch for workers while you are riding in the car.

 Tell Me More:

United States Telephone
   Association
1401 H St. NW, Suite 600
Washington, DC 20005-2136

Communication Workers of America
Dept. of Apprenticeships, Benefits,
   and Employment
501 3rd St. NW
Washington, DC 20001

Millwrights

Millwrights must install machinery in accordance with precise specifications

 Education and Training:

A high school diploma with a four-year on-the-job training program is usually preferred.

 Job Outlook:

Good

 Average Earnings:

Medium

What They Do: Millwrights install, repair, service, replace, and take apart heavy equipment and machinery used in many industries. When moving heavy machinery, millwrights need to know what works best for the job. They might use cables, cranes, hydraulic lift trucks, or other means. Millwrights use special tools and metalworking equipment in their job. They often work with computer and electronic experts when installing new equipment.

Working Conditions: Millwrights jobs vary depending where they work. Overtime is needed during busy production times. Safety belts and hard hats are usually worn for safety.

Related Jobs: Industrial machinery repairer, aircraft mechanic, diesel mechanic, and farm equipment mechanic

Subjects To Study Now and Later: English, mathematics, computer operations, mechanics, drafting, physics, and shop

Getting Ready and Places to Go to Observe: Working with electrical and electronic projects gives you an idea of what millwrights do on a larger scale. Do you know of industries in your area that use heavy machinery and equipment in production? They will usually have a millwright working there.

 Tell Me More:

The National Tooling and
    Machining Association
9300 Livingston Road
Fort Washington, MD 20744

Small-Engine Mechanics

Routine maintenance is a major part of the small-engine mechanic's work.

Education and Training:

Mechanical training in high school, vocational and technical school, or a community college is preferred.

Job Outlook:

Poor

Average Earnings:

Low

What They Do: Small-engine mechanics repair and service engines that are smaller than engines in cars and trucks. These engines are used in things like boats, lawn mowers, and power saws. Small-engine mechanics do routine maintenance, such as cleaning and replacing worn parts. When a breakdown occurs, the mechanic finds and repairs the problem. Mechanics usually service and repair one type of engine.

Working Conditions: Small-engine mechanics usually work indoors in repair shops that are well lighted. Those who work on motorboats may work outdoors in all kinds of weather.

Related Jobs: Automotive mechanic, diesel mechanic, farm equipment mechanic, and mobile heavy equipment mechanic

Subjects To Study Now and Later: Mechanics, electronics, welding, metalworking, drafting, mathematics, and English

Getting Ready and Places to Go to Observe: You can learn how an engine works by reading books and magazines available at your library. Older teenagers often learn about engines by working on them. Working on engines is a hobby for many people. Do you know anyone who enjoys working on cars? Ask this person to explain the parts of an engine and how a car works.

Tell Me More:

Motorcycle Mechanics Institute
2844 West Deer Valley Rd.
Phoenix, AZ 85027

Outdoor Power Equipment Institute
341 South Patrick St.
Alexandria, VA 22314

This page is Blank

Construction
Trades
Occupations

Workers in this cluster construct, alter, and maintain buildings and other structures.
They may operate drilling and mining equipment. They must be able to follow plans.
Courses in school to help prepare for these jobs include mathematics, shop, and drafting.

Bricklayers

 Education and Training:

A high school diploma and three years on-the-job training programs are recommended. Many receive training in vocational educational schools.

Self-employed bricklayers specialize in small jobs like patios, walks, and fireplaces.

 Job Outlook:

Good

 Average Earnings:

Medium

What They Do: Bricklayers build parts of buildings and homes with brick, concrete block, and other brick-like materials. It takes special skills and experience to be able to do a job that is attractive and built to last. Bricklayers use special tools to make their job easier. They often have helpers that do many jobs including mixing mortar and carrying bricks.

Working Conditions: Bricklayers work outdoors and sometimes indoors. They lift heavy materials, bend, stand, and kneel a lot.

Related Jobs: Concrete mason, plasterer, terrazzo worker, and tilesetter

Subjects To Study Now and Later: English, mathematics, electronics, carpentry, physics, and drafting

Getting Ready and Places to Go to Observe: There are several craft kits available that show you how to do tile projects. Look for "how-to" books at the library that give other building ideas. Check your newspaper or telephone directory for a listing of bricklayers that work close to you. Ask if you can watch them at work.

 Tell Me More:

Brick Institute of America
11490 Commerce Park Dr.
Reston, VA 22091-1525

National Concrete Masonry
  Association
2302 Horse Pen Rd.
Herndon, VA 22071

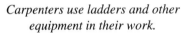
Carpenters use ladders and other equipment in their work.

Education and Training:

A high school education and on-the-job training are recommended. Many receive training through vocational education or employer training programs.

Job Outlook:

Excellent

Average Earnings:

Low - Medium

What They Do: Carpenters build structures and buildings with wood and other materials. They have different duties depending on the type of job. Carpenters start by using blueprints to help them measure and plan how to begin the job. They cut materials and put them together with nails and screws. They use special tools like levels and framing squares.

Working Conditions: Carpenters' work requires lifting, standing, and working both indoors and outdoors. Safety is a factor when using sharp tools and power equipment. Working in different locations is required.

Related Jobs: Bricklayer, electrician, pipefitter, plumber, and stonemason

Subjects To Study Now and Later: English, mathematics, electronics, drafting, shop, and welding

Getting Ready and Places to Go to Observe: Build your own small structure using wood scraps and other materials that you can find. Find or draw instructions and follow them. Measure the pieces and, with an adult, cut them to the right length. Join the materials together with screws, nails, or glue. Check your project to be sure you followed the directions correctly. Watch for new homes and buildings under construction in your area. Be sure to get permission before entering a construction area. If you drive by often, watch for different jobs that carpenters do in each phase of construction.

Tell Me More:

Associated Builders and
   Contractors
1300 North 17th St.
Rosslyn, VA 22209

Associated General Contractors of
   America, Inc.
1957 E St. NW
Washington, DC 20006

Carpet Installers

The majority of carpet installers are self-employed.

  Education and Training:

A high school diploma and one to four years on-the-job training is recommended.

 Job Outlook:

Good

 Average Earnings:

Medium

What They Do: Carpet installers cut and lay carpet. They measure, clean and check the floor, put down tack or tape, and lay the pad. Then the carpet is installed using special tools like carpet knives, knee kickers, and power stretchers.

Working Conditions: Carpet installers work indoors. This job requires lifting and working in many positions like kneeling, bending, and reaching.

Related Jobs: Carpenter, drywall installer, painter, roofer, and tilesetter

Subjects To Study Now and Later: English, mathematics, electronics, carpentry, shop, and drafting

Getting Ready and Places to Go to Observe: Take a close look at the carpet in your home or school. Can you tell where the carpet was cut and pieced together? Retail stores that sell carpet have samples of different kinds of carpet and pad for sale. Ask if some types are harder to install than others. Find out how many carpet installers work for them.

 Tell Me More:

Floor Covering Installation
    Contractors Association
P.O. Box 948
Dalton, GA 30722-0948

United Brotherhood of Carpenters
    and Joiners of America
101 Constitution Ave. NW
Washington, DC 20001

Concrete Masons

Concrete masons trowel the concrete back and forth to make a smooth surface.

Education and Training:

A high school diploma is preferred for this job. On-the-job training or a two- to three-year formal training program is required.

Job Outlook:

Poor

Average Earnings:

Low - Medium

What They Do: Concrete masons place and finish concrete for many different types of jobs. Concrete is used for dams, roads, walls and sidewalks. Concrete masons place boards or metal in the shape of how the concrete will be when completed. Once the concrete is poured into the board or metal forms, they use special tools to spread, level, and smooth the surface of the concrete.

Working Conditions: Concrete masons usually work outdoors. They bend and kneel a lot. They cannot work outdoors during freezing and rainy weather.

Related Jobs: Bricklayer, form builder, marble setter, plasterers, stonemason, and tilesetter

Subjects To Study Now and Later: English, mathematics, electronics, carpentry, and drafting

Getting Ready and Places to Go to Observe: Study more about concrete masons in books from the library. Find books for your age level that have fun, easy to do projects and instructions that include mixing and using materials that are like concrete. Watch for new roads and buildings that concrete masons will be working on.

Tell Me More:

Associated General
  Contractors of America
1957 E St. NW
Washington, DC 20006

International Union of Bricklayers
  and Allied Craftsmen
International Masonry Institute
Apprenticeship and Training
815 15th St. NW, Suite 1001
Washington, DC 20005

Drywall Workers

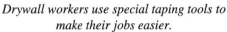

Drywall workers use special taping tools to make their jobs easier.

Education and Training:

A high school diploma and on-the-job training or a two-year formal training program is required for this job.

Job Outlook:

Good

Average Earnings:

Low - Medium

What They Do: Drywall workers fasten drywall sheets or panels to walls and ceilings in homes and other buildings. They prepare the panels for painting. Special tools are used to cut, install, and finish the drywall. Some drywall workers apply texture to the finished walls with spray guns and other tools.

Working Conditions: Drywall workers do their job indoors. They stand, bend, and lift heavy panels. Sometimes they wear masks for safety reasons when sanding. They must be alert when working in high places and on ladders.

Related Jobs: Carpenter, floor covering installer, form builder, insulation worker, and plasterer

Subjects To Study Now and Later: English, mathematics, shop, carpentry, welding, and drafting

Getting Ready and Places to Go to Observe: Find three different types of finished drywall jobs in homes and buildings. How is the texture different? Visit retail stores in your area that sell drywall sheets, tools and supplies.

Tell Me More:

Associated Builders and
    Contractors, Inc.
1300 N. 17th St.
Rosslyn, VA 22209

United Brotherhood of
    Carpenters and Joiners of
    America
101 Constitution Ave. NW
Washington, DC 20001

Electricians

  ## Education and Training:

A high school diploma and four to five years additional training is required for this job.

 ## Job Outlook:

Excellent

  ## Average Earnings:

Medium

Electricians often must work in awkward positions and risk injury from electrical shocks, falls, and cuts.

What They Do: Electricians install, maintain and repair electrical systems. They must follow national, state, and local building codes when installing new systems. Some electricians also install electronic controls (like thermostats), and telephone or computer wiring. Electricians use special tools and testing equipment in their job.

Working Conditions: Electricians work in many different positions like standing, bending, and working on ladders. They need to be careful to avoid injury from falling or electrical shock. Some electricians work nights and weekends.

Related Jobs: Heating and air conditioning mechanic, cable installer, electronic repairer, and elevator contractor

Subjects To Study Now and Later: English, mathematics, electronics, drafting, and physics

Getting Ready and Places to Go to Observe: Study about electricity from the time it was invented until today. Make a list of safety rules to follow when using electrical appliances. Share it with others. Local utility companies often have tours available. Can you think of a place where you go that does not use electricity?

 Tell Me More:

Independent Electrical
   Contractors, Inc.
507 Wythe St.
Alexandria, VA 22314

National Electrical Contractors
   Association
3 Metro Center, Suite 1100
Bethesda, MD 20814

Glaziers

 Education and Training:

A high school diploma is preferred with a 3- to 4-year on-the-job training program.

 Job Outlook:

Poor

 Average Earnings:

Medium

Glaziers may be injured by broken glass, falls, or from improperly lifting of glass.

What They Do: Glaziers select, cut, install and remove glass. They also do other jobs like installing mirrors and shower doors. They use glasscutters, glazing knives, and other special tools in their trade. Glaziers work in many places including large commercial buildings, homes, and skyscrapers.

Working Conditions: This job requires heavy lifting, bending, kneeling and standing. Sometimes glaziers work in high places. Safety measures must be used at all times when working with broken glass.

Related Jobs: Bricklayer, carpenter, floor layer, paperhanger, terrazzo worker, and tilesetter

Subjects To Study Now and Later: English, mathematics, mechanical drawing, shop, and physics

Getting Ready and Places to Go to Observe: Kits are available that have the necessary supplies, tools, and directions that allow youth to be able (while working with an adult) to make a project using glass. Retail stores that sell windows or glass in your area are good places to visit and talk to glaziers about their job.

 Tell Me More:

National Glass Association
Education and Training Dept.
8200 Greensboro Drive, 3rd Floor
McLean, VA 22102

Flat Glass Marketing Association
White Lakes Professional Building
3310 Southwest Harrison St.
Topeka, KS 66611-2279

Insulation Workers

Education and Training:

A high school diploma is preferred. Training programs are available.

Job Outlook:

Excellent

Average Earnings:

Medium - High

A high turnover rate of insulation worker jobs keeps job openings plentiful.

What They Do: Insulation workers cut, fit, and install insulating material. Insulation is used in building and over pipes to keep heat in during the winter and out in the summer. Insulation is installed by using cement, staples, wire, tape, or spray. Common hand tools like brushes, knives, scissors, and saws are used.

Working Conditions: Insulation workers stand, bend, and kneel most of the work day. Small particles from the insulation are irritating to eyes, skin, and the respiratory system so safety precautions must be taken and special clothing worn.

Related Jobs: Carpenter, carpet installer, roofer, and sheet-metal worker

Subjects To Study Now and Later: English, mathematics, mechanics, carpentry, drafting, and welding

Getting Ready and Places to Go to Observe: Read about energy conservation to learn why insulating is important. Talk to your librarian to get other books on this subject. Buildings and homes under construction hire insulation workers. Contact local contractors or check the telephone directory for numbers of local insulation workers that you can call for more information.

Tell Me More:

National Insulation and Abatement
 Contractors Association
99 Canal Center Plaza, Suite 222
Alexandria, VA 22314

Insulation Contractors Association
 of America
1321 Duke St., Suite 303
Alexandria, VA 22314

Painters

Painters fill cracks and smooth surfaces prior to painting.

 Education and Training:

A high school education is needed to begin a three-year training program. Some painters learn on-the-job.

 Job Outlook:

Good

 Average Earnings:

Low

What They Do: Painters use brushes, rollers, sprayers and other special tools to apply paint. Painters also apply different finishes like varnish and stains. They paint inside and outside on buildings and other structures. It is necessary to choose the right kind of paint and tools to do the job. Each surface must be properly prepared before starting.

Working Conditions: Painters stand, climb, and bend a lot in their job. They need to work with their arms overhead for long periods of time. Sometimes masks are worn for safety.

Related Jobs: Billboard posterer, metal sprayer, undercoater and transportation equipment painter

Subjects To Study Now and Later: English, mathematics, electronics, carpentry, physics, and drafting

Getting Ready and Places to Go to Observe: Find a small project that you can paint. There are "how to" books at the library that give directions on preparation, painting, and cleanup. Always work with an adult. Visit a store in your area that specializes in selling paint and supplies. They can explain about the different types of paint and supplies available.

 Tell Me More:

Associated Builders and Contractors
1300 N. 17th St.
Rosslyn, VA 22209

International Brotherhood of
   Painters and Allied Trades
1750 New York Ave. NW
Washington, DC 20006

Plasterers can create different effects that cannot be done with drywall.

Education and Training:

A high school diploma is preferred before training on-the-job or beginning a two- to three-year training program.

Job Outlook:

Good

Average Earnings:

Medium - High

What They Do: Plasterers apply plaster to interior walls, ceilings, and exterior surfaces. They may also cast ornamental designs by using molds. Plasterers mix different types of plaster depending on the type of surface needed and they use special tools to apply the plaster.

Working Conditions: A plasterer must stand, bend, lift, and reach overhead. They sometimes work high off the ground on scaffolds.

Related Jobs: Drywall finisher, bricklayer, concrete mason, stonemason, and tilesetter

Subjects To Study Now and Later: English, mathematics, shop, mechanical drawing, and physics

Getting Ready and Places to Go to Observe: There are kits available at craft stores that teach you how to mold plaster to make ornamental designs. "How to" books from the library will teach you more about this career. New construction areas near you may be using plasterers to finish interior or exterior walls. The telephone directory will list plasterers in your area.

Tell Me More:

International Union of Bricklayers
   and Allied Craftsman
815 15th St. NW
Washington, DC 20005

Operative Plasterers' and Cement
   Masons' Association
1125 17th St. NW
Washington, DC 20036

Plumbers

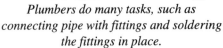
Plumbers do many tasks, such as connecting pipe with fittings and soldering the fittings in place.

 Education and Training:

Most plumbers have a high school diploma followed by a training program that takes four to five years.

 Job Outlook:

Excellent

 Average Earnings:

Medium

What They Do: Plumbers install, maintain, and repair the water, waste disposal, drainage, and other systems in buildings and homes. They also install fixtures, sinks, toilets, and appliances. Plumbers need to know about the different types of pipe and ways to install each type. They need to be able to read blueprints when installing new systems.

Working Conditions: Plumbers stand, kneel, and sometimes work in small places. They work indoors and outdoors in all kinds of weather. Plumbers need to work safely when on ladders or using special tools.

Related Jobs: Boilermaker, electrician, millwright, sheet-metal worker, and heating, air-conditioning and refrigeration mechanic

Subjects To Study Now and Later: English, mathematics, shop, physics, and drafting

Getting Ready and Places to Go to Observe: Study the water pipe system where you live. Draw plans (blueprints) of how you think the system is designed. Ask an adult if you can look at actual blueprints. Visit hardware stores to find out about the many types of pipe, fittings, and other supplies that plumbers use. Plumbers work at new construction sites and also repair existing water systems. Check the newspaper or telephone directory to talk with plumbers that work in your area.

 Tell Me More:

National Association of Plumbing-
Heating-Cooling Contractors
P.O. Box 6808
Falls Church, VA 22046

Associated Builders and
 Contractors
1300 N. 17th St.
Rosslyn, VA 22209

Roofers

Education and Training:

A high school education is helpful. Roofers learn the trade on-the-job or in a training program that includes classroom instruction.

Job Outlook:

Excellent

Good physical condition and good balance are important for roofers.

Average Earnings:

Low - Medium

What They Do: Roofers install new roofs and replace or repair existing roofs. Roofers work on either flat or slanted roof types. Flat roofs have several layers of materials and slanted roofs have shingles. Some roofers also waterproof foundation floors and walls.

Working Conditions: Roofers work outdoors in all kinds of weather. This type of work requires lifting, climbing, bending, and working on ladders. Safety measures must be used at all times because this job has a high accident rate.

Related Jobs: Carpenter, concrete mason, drywall worker, plasterer, and tilesetter

Subjects To Study Now and Later: English, mathematics, shop, mechanical drawing, carpentry, and drafting

Getting Ready and Places to Go to Observe: Visit a hardware store that sells roofing and supplies to take a close look at the different types of roofing materials that roofers use. Watch for roofers at work on different types of homes and buildings in your area. Make a note of how many workers are doing a job. How long do you think it will take to finish. What type of materials and tools are they using?

Tell Me More:

National Roofing Contractors
   Association
10255 W. Higgins Rd.
Rosemont, IL 60018

United Union of Roofers,
   Waterproofers & Allied Workers
1125 17th St. NW
Washington, DC 20036

Sheetmetal Workers

Education and Training:

The way most sheetmetal workers learn their trade is by attending a school program that provides four to five years of on-the-job training and classroom courses.

Job Outlook:

Good

Average Earnings:

Medium - High

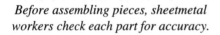

Before assembling pieces, sheetmetal workers check each part for accuracy.

What They Do: Sheetmetal workers make, install, and maintain sheet-metal products. They make products for heating and air conditioning systems, roofs, siding, rain gutters, and many other uses. Some workers use computerized equipment. Others use hand calculators to figure the layout of each product. Some jobs are started in the shop and finished at the job, while others are done completely at the job site.

Working Conditions: Sheetmetal workers work in shops and at job sites. This job requires standing, lifting, bending, and climbing. Safety practices are needed when working with machinery and sharp metal.

Related Jobs: Glazier, heating and air conditioning technician, machinist, metal fabricator, tool and die maker

Subjects To Study Now and Later: English, mathematics, drafting, mechanical drawing, and shop

Getting Ready and Places to Go to Observe: Learning to use a computer and doing well in mathematics will give you skills that will be useful in this career. Most sheetmetal workers are employed by plumbing, and heating and air-conditioning contractors. Check your telephone directory for contractors in your area. Watch for new homes and buildings under construction. They will probably be using sheetmetal products in the construction.

Tell Me More:

The Sheet Metal National Training Fund
601 N. Fairfax St., Suite 240
Alexandria, VA 22314

Structural Ironworkers

 Education and Training:

Three years in a formal training program with classroom instruction is required.

 Job Outlook:

Poor

 Average Earnings:

Medium

Structural ironworkers' work can be limited by bad weather and short term construction jobs.

What They Do: Structural ironworkers help build highways, bridges, large buildings, and many other structures. First they build the steel frames of the structure. The steel provides additional strength. They also assemble and operate large equipment, such as cranes, which are used to move the steel, buckets of concrete, lumber, and other materials used at the construction site. Ironworkers then connect columns, beams, and other steel pieces of the building. They must follow blueprints and instructions from managers.

Working Conditions: Structural ironworkers work outdoors in all kinds of weather. Many also work at great heights.

Related Jobs: Reinforcing ironworker, engineer, concrete mason, and welder

Subjects To Study Now and Later: Mathematics, shop, mechanical drawing, and English

Getting Ready and Places to Go to Observe: Using a computer or paper, try drawing the parts that might be needed to build an office building or a bridge. Drive by a construction site. Are you able to see the parts that help strengthen the building?

 Tell Me More:

Associated General Contractors
  of America, Inc.
1300 N 17th St.
Rosslyn, VA 22209-3883

National Erectors Association
1501 Lee Hwy., Suite 202
Arlington, VA 22209

Tilesetters

  Education and Training:

A three-year training program after high school is recommended.

 Job Outlook:

Poor

 Average Earnings:

Medium

Tilesetters use their knowledge along with skill to produce attractive, durable surfaces.

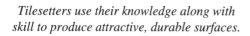

What They Do: Tilesetters apply tile to floors, walls, and ceilings. To set tile, they use cement or a very sticky paste, called mastic. There are many steps the tilesetter must do to finish a job. Tilesetting was once an ancient art form. It still requires a great deal of skill to do a tile job well. Many tilesetters are self-employed.

Working Conditions: Tilesetters usually work indoors. They use tools to set the tile. They must bend, kneel, and reach a lot.

Related Jobs: Bricklayer, concrete mason, marblesetter, plasterer, stonemason, and terrazzo worker

Subjects To Study Now and Later: Mathematics, mechanical drawing, shop, art, and English

Getting Ready and Places to Go to Observe: Part of being a good tilesetter is developing a good eye for tile design and color. Look at the many decorating magazines available in libraries and supermarkets for tile designs and ideas. Ask friends and neighbors if they have ever set tile.

 Tell Me More:

International Union of Bricklayers and Allied Craftsmen
International Masonry Institute/Apprenticeship & Training
823 15th St. NW
Washington, DC 20005

Production and Laborers Occupations

Workers in these occupations set up, install, adjust, operate, and tend machinery and equipment. They use handtools and power tools to put together products. They must be accurate in their work.

Precision Assemblers

Precision assemblers must pay attention to detail while working quickly.

 Education and Training:

A high school diploma is helpful. Some technical school or military training is required. Many are trained on-the-job.

 Job Outlook:

Poor

 Average Earnings:

Low

What They Do: Precision assemblers put together parts which become a finished product. Precision assemblers must be very accurate in how they put the parts together. Some work on assembling the parts of a car. Others assemble electrical or electronic equipment, like computers or radar equipment. There are others who work on machines such as engines or printing machines. Some precision assemblers work on aircraft. They put together parts of airplanes, like wings. Reading engineering instructions and using special tools and measuring instruments are important skills for this job.

Working Conditions: Precision assemblers work indoors in manufacturing plants. It depends on the type of manufacturing plant whether they work at clean tables or with greasy and heavy objects.

Related Jobs: Welder, ophthalmic laboratory technician, and machine operator

Subjects To Study Now and Later: English, mathematics, electronics, drafting, biology, physics, chemistry, mechanics, and computer science

Getting Ready and Places to Go to Observe: Read about how things work. There are books available at libraries that tell how mechanical, electronic, and many other types of things work. Find out what kind of manufacturing plants are in your area. Contact them and ask the personnel department if they employ precision assemblers. They may be able to give you more information about this job.

 Tell Me More:

Contact a state employment office for information about job requirements in your area.

Fishers

Education and Training:

Usually on-the-job training is all that is needed. There are some two-year and bachelor's programs.

Fishers work outdoors in all kinds of weather.

Job Outlook:

Poor

Average Earnings:

Low - High

What They Do: Fishers gather marine life for many uses. The most common use is to supply food for people and animals. Most fishers work on motorboats in shallow waters and often in sight of land. There are usually just one or two fishers on the boat. The fishers place nets and other tools in rivers, lakes, and bays. Some fishers scuba dive to gather shellfish, coral and sponges. When gathering sea life hundreds of miles from shore, large fishing boats with many fishers are used. Some fishers rent their vessels (boats) to groups for sport fishing.

Working Conditions: Fishers work outdoors at all times. They work in all kinds of weather. Some fishing trips take weeks or months away from home.

Related Jobs: Fish caretaker, fish farmer, fishing guide, fish hatchery worker, fish warden, harbor pilot, and shellfish grower

Subjects To Study Now and Later: English, biology, and physical education

Getting Ready and Places to Go to Observe: Go fishing. There are lots of differences between saltwater and freshwater fishing. If you have the chance, try both. You can also read about all the many types of life in water. In addition, to fish, there are plants, coral, and many other types of animals. If you live near any lakes, rivers or the ocean where fishers are working, you can watch them when they get ready to leave shore and when they return.

Tell Me More:

Marine Technology Society
1828 L St. NW, Suite 906
Washington, DC 20036-5104

National Marine Fisheries Service
NMFS Scientific Publications Office
7600 Sand Point Way NE
Seattle, WA 98115

Logging Workers

Education and Training:
Most training is on-the-job. Some schools and colleges have forestry programs.

Job Outlook:
Good

Average Earnings:
Low

Most logging operations are concentrated in the Southeast and Northwest parts of the country.

What They Do: Logging workers harvest timber which is used for many different products. Some are called fallers. They cut down trees with chain saws and other tools. Others are called choker setters. These workers fasten chains around logs which are dragged by tractors to an area called a landing. Logging tractor operators drive tractors which drag logs to a landing. Workers who get the logs off the chains at the landing are called riggers. There are many other workers who contribute to harvesting timber from the Nation's forests.

Working Conditions: Logging workers work outdoors in all kinds of weather. They must do a lot of lifting, climbing and other physical activities.

Related Jobs: Arborist, groundskeeper, nursery worker, gardener, and soil conservation technician

Subjects To Study Now and Later: English, mathematics, biology, physical education, and mechanics

Getting Ready and Places to Go to Observe: Learn about the many kinds of trees near where you live. Visit a nursery to see various types. Camping is a fun way to learn about the forests and the natural wildlife near you.

Tell Me More:

Northeastern Loggers Association
P.O. Box 69
Old Forge, NY 13420

Chief, US Forest Service
U.S. Dept. of Agriculture
14th St. and Independence Ave. SW
Washington, DC 20013

Butchers

Education and Training:

Some butchers learn basic skills at trade and vocational schools. Most train on-the-job.

Job Outlook:

Poor

Average Earnings:

Low

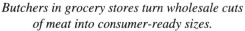
Butchers in grocery stores turn wholesale cuts of meat into consumer-ready sizes.

What They Do: Butchers cut large pieces of meat and chicken into smaller sections for people to buy. Some butchers work in meatpacking plants. Butchers in meatpacking plants work in assembly lines. They cut large pieces which are sent to wholesalers and grocery stores. Wholesalers supply meat to large buyers of meat and poultry, such as restaurants. Butchers in grocery stores and wholesalers also cut the large pieces of meat into small pieces, called cuts, which are the right size for people to cook. Butchers use knives, meat saws, and other sharp equipment.

Working Conditions: Butchers usually work indoors in refrigerated rooms to prevent meat and poultry from spoiling. The work areas must be clean and sanitary. They stand for long periods of time.

Related Jobs: Baker, chef, cook, and food preparation worker

Subjects To Study Now and Later: Mechanics, biology, English, and agriculture

Getting Ready and Places to Go to Observe: Help your parents as they prepare dinner. It is important to have clean hands and a clean work area. If your family cooks a whole turkey or chicken, watch how they clean and carve it after cooking. Sometimes grocery stores give tours of the meat department where the butchers work. Find out if the grocery store where your family shops will give you a tour. Look at all the different cuts of meat available to buy.

Tell Me More:

United Food and Commercial Workers Int'l Union
1775 K St. NW
Washington, DC 20006

Jewelers

Education and Training:

A technical school is where jewelers' skills are usually learned. It takes six months to three years to complete. Some learn on-the-job.

Job Outlook:

Poor

Average Earnings:

Low - Medium

Many of the materials jewelers work with are very valuable.

What They Do: Jewelers make, repair and alter jewelry. They use different materials including precious metals and stones, such as gold and diamonds. Many tools are used, such as drills, pliers, saws, and special handtools. Some jewelers specialize in an area of the jewelry field. It could be designing, gem cutting, repair, sales or appraisal. Some are involved in all these areas. Jewelers who work in manufacturing may set stones or make models to shape the metal.

Working Conditions: Jewelers work indoors in comfortable areas. They may sit for long periods of time. In retail stores, they talk to customers.

Related Jobs: Polisher, gemcutter, hand engraver, and watch maker and repairer

Subjects To Study Now and Later: Art, mathematics, mechanical drawing, chemistry, and English

Getting Ready and Places to Go to Observe: You can start designing jewelry by drawing sketches on paper. Another way to design jewelry is to bead necklaces and bracelets. Beads are available at many art and craft stores.

Tell Me More:

Jewelers of America
1185 Avenue of the Americas
30th Floor
New York, NY 10036

Gemological Institute of America
5345 Armada Dr.
Carlsbad, CA 92008
http://www.gia.org

Education and Training:

Training programs with classroom instruction and training on-the-job is the most common way for machinists to learn their trade.

Job Outlook:

Poor

Average Earnings:

Medium

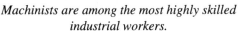

Machinists are among the most highly skilled industrial workers.

What They Do: Machinists make metal parts. These parts must be carefully made exactly to the specifications ordered. Machinists make these parts in small amounts or maybe only one will be made. They operate many different types of machine tools and use different kinds of metals like steel, aluminum, and brass. Some machinists also repair and make new parts for older machinery.

Working Conditions: Machinists work indoors. They wear special safety equipment, like earplugs and safety glasses. This job requires lifting and standing for long periods. Evenings, weekends, and overtime is common.

Related Jobs: Toolmaker, tool programmer, instrument maker, blacksmith, gunsmith, welder, and patternmaker

Subjects To Study Now and Later: English, mathematics, drafting, blueprint reading, electronics, and computer operations

Getting Ready and Places to Go to Observe: Studying about machinery, using the computer, and building projects using tools help in learning about the jobs that machinists do. Machinists work in small machine shops or for large manufacturing companies like metalworking, industrial, aircraft, or motor vehicle firms. Most machinists work in towns and cities where there is a lot of manufacturing.

Tell Me More:

The Precision Machined Products
   Association
6700 West Snowville Rd.
Brecksville, OH 44141

The National Tooling and
   Machining Association
9300 Livingston Rd.
Fort Washington, MD 20744

Tool and Die Makers

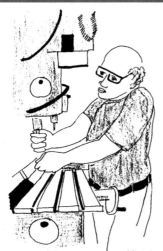

Most employers report difficulty in finding skilled tool and die makers.

 Education and Training:

A high school and vocational education is preferred. Most learn with a combination of classroom education and on-the-job training, which usually takes 4 - 5 years.

 Job Outlook:

Good

 Average Earnings:

Medium

What They Do: Tool and die makers make tools, dies, and special parts that are used in machines. They are highly skilled workers. The tools and dies they make are used to cut and shape metal and other material. They use many types of machine and measuring tools. They must also know the differences about working with many metals. Tool and die makers work from blueprints or instructions. They measure and mark the metal that will be cut. The cutting, drilling, assembling, and other work they do on the part must be very accurate.

Working Conditions: Tool and die makers work indoors in tool rooms. They stand a lot and may do heavy lifting. Tool and die makers must wear safety glasses and earplugs.

Related Jobs: Machinist, mold maker, instrument maker, metalworking machine operator, tool programmer, blacksmith, locksmith, and welder

Subjects To Study Now and Later: English, mathematics, machine shop, metalworking, and drafting

Getting Ready and Places to Go to Observe: Books from the library can teach you more about machines. Find a broken machine that can be taken apart so you can see the different parts. High schools have machine shop classes that you can observe to learn more about this career.

 Tell Me More:

The Precision Machined Products
   Association
6700 West Snowville Rd.
Brecksville, OH 44141

The National Tooling and
   Machining Association
9300 Livingston Rd.
Ft. Washington, MD 20744

Education and Training:

Formal training in high school is available. Many vocational schools, community colleges, and the Armed Forces offer training for this highly skilled job.

Job Outlook:

Good

Average Earnings:

Low - Medium

Welders wear protective gear for welding metals in various production and repair tasks.

What They Do: Welders use special welding equipment to join metal parts together. They use heat to melt the pieces and fuse them together. Some things are welded by hand and others are welded by an automatic machine that the welder operates and manages.

Working Conditions: Welders wear special clothing, helmets with protective lenses, and other safety gear. They may be exposed to the toxic gases that some metals give off when they melt. Welders work in many positions like bending and kneeling.

Related Jobs: Blacksmith, machine-tool operator, tool-and-die maker, millwright, and sheet-metal worker

Subjects To Study Now and Later: English, shop, mechanics, mathematics, and electronics

Getting Ready and Places to Go to Observe: Welding is used on many different things like automobiles, bridges, and ships. Can you find something that has been welded together? Read more about welding in books from the library. Welders often work in plants that make motor vehicles or other metal products. They also may work for firms that construct bridges or large buildings. Ask an adult to help you find out what welders do in your area.

Tell Me More:

American Welding Society
550 N.W. Lejeune Rd.
Miami, FL 33126-5699

Career College Association
750 1st St. NE, Suite 900
Washington, DC 20002

Water Treatment Plant Operators

Water treatment plant operators take water samples.

 Education and Training:

At least a high school diploma is required. There are one- and two-year programs also available.

 Job Outlook:

Excellent

 Average Earnings:

Low - Medium

What They Do: Water treatment plant operators treat water so that it is safe to drink. The water comes from rivers, streams, and wells. Water treatment plant operators control and repair the equipment which removes unhealthy things from water. Computers are being used more to monitor this equipment.

Working Conditions: Water treatment plant operators work both indoors and outdoors. They are around noisy equipment and unpleasant odors. They sometimes work nights, weekends, and holidays.

Related Jobs: Boiler operator, gas compressor operator, power plant operator, power reactor operator, stationary engineer, turbine operator, and petroleum refinery operator

Subjects To Study Now and Later: Mathematics, chemistry, biology, computer science, and English

Getting Ready and Places to Go to Observe: Read what you can about water from books in the library. Contact a community college or vocational technical school to find out if they have classes in water technology that can provide you with information.

 Tell Me More:

Association of Boards of Certification
208 Fifth St.
Ames, IA 50010-6259

American Waterworks Association
6666 West Quincy
Denver, CO 80235

Desktop Publishing Specialists

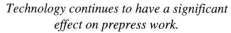
Technology continues to have a significant effect on prepress work.

Education and Training:

High school graduates with good communication, computer, and mathematical skills are preferred.

Job Outlook:

Excellent

Average Earnings:

Medium

What They Do: Desktop publishing specialists prepare material for printing presses. Special desktop publishing software programs are used on computers to arrange artwork and type. The computer screen shows how the page will look when it is printed. When this is completed, the work of the desktop publishing specialist is reviewed for overall quality and then sent to the production department to start the printing process. Many small business owners do their own desktop publishing instead of hiring a specialist.

Working Conditions: Desktop publishing specialists work in clean offices. They work on computers most of the day.

Related Jobs: Preflight technician, typesetter, sign painter, graphic artist, scanner operator, and job printer

Subjects To Study Now and Later: English, mathematics, computers, keyboarding, art, and speech

Getting Ready and Places to Go to Observe: If you have access to a computer and a desktop publishing program, learn how to use it. There are many books available to help as you learn. Take a brochure or any printed piece of paper and try to duplicate it on the computer. If you don't have a computer and software, read as much as you can about graphic art and design.

Tell Me More:

Education Council of the Graphic
   Arts Industry
1899 Preston White Dr.
Reston, VA 20191

The Graphic Arts Technical
   Foundation
200 Deer Run Road
Sewickley, PA 15143

Printing Press Operators

Printing press operators inspect sheets to check for imperfections.

 Education and Training:

In the coming years formal training in classes, as well as work experience, will be expected.

 Job Outlook:

Poor

 Average Earnings:

Low - Medium

What They Do: Printing press operators are responsible for the preparation and operation of presses. Printing press operators must make sure that paper and ink are correct. They monitor the press as paper runs through it. Their eyesight must be good. If they work with different colored inks, they need to be able to see slight differences in color.

Working Conditions: Printing press operators work indoors and stand on their feet most of the time. Many work evenings and over 40 hours a week.

Related Jobs: Papermaking machine operator, shoemaking machine operator, bindery machine operator, and precision machine operator

Subjects To Study Now and Later: Chemistry, electronics, art, print shop, physics, and English

Getting Ready and Places to Go to Observe: Read books about printing. A good one to look for at your library is "The Pocket Pal." There are printers in every community. Go to a local small print company and ask if you can have a tour. Also visit a large print company if you have one near you. What differences in the equipment do you notice?

 Tell Me More:

The Graphic Arts Technical Foundation
200 Deer Run Road
Sewickley, PA 15143

PIA - Printing Industries of America, Inc.
100 Daingerfield Rd.
Alexandria, VA 22314

Apparel Workers

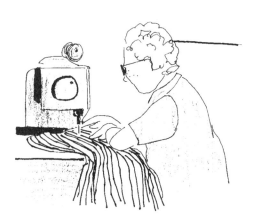

Apparel workers use a variety of tools and materials.

Education and Training:

On-the-job training is often available to begin work as an apparel worker. A high school diploma and vocational training is recommended for advancement to supervisor positions.

Job Outlook:

Poor

Average Earnings:

Low

What They Do: Apparel workers make clothing and other items using cloth. They design an item and make a pattern. They cut the cloth using the pattern. Most of the sewing is done by machine operators. When the sewing is finished, apparel workers remove any loose threads and inspect the item.

Working Conditions: Apparel workers who work in factories may sit or stand for long periods of time. Others work for laundromats or retail places that require evening and weekend hours.

Related Jobs: Shoe and leather worker, precision woodworker, upholsterer, metalworking and plastics-working machine operator

Subjects To Study Now and Later: Mathematics, electronics, blueprint reading, English, and shop

Getting Ready and Places to Go to Observe: Using "how to" books from the library, make a simple piece of clothing from scraps of fabric you have at home. Make a pattern, cut it out, and stitch the item by hand. This will give you an idea of the work apparel workers do on the job. Some apparel workers are custom tailors or sewers. They work in retail clothing stores. Contact a clothing store in your area and ask if they hire a tailor or sewer.

Tell Me More:

American Apparel Manufacturers
    Association
250 Wilson Blvd., Suite 301
Arlington, VA 22201

Leather Workers

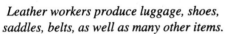

Leather workers produce luggage, shoes, saddles, belts, as well as many other items.

Education and Training:

On-the-job training is the most common way leather workers learn their craft. Some schools offer vocational training programs.

Job Outlook:

Poor

Average Earnings:

Low - Medium

What They Do: Leather workers design and make products out of leather. They trace a pattern onto leather, cut, and sew the pieces together. They use machines and handtools, like knives and hammers, to make the job easier.

Working Conditions: Leather workers' job duties and working conditions vary depending on the size of the factory or business. Some work evenings and weekends.

Related Jobs: Dressmaker, designer, patternmaker, and furrier

Subjects To Study Now and Later: English, mathematics, shop, and mechanics

Getting Ready and Places to Go to Observe: Craft kits that teach you how to make leather projects are available at craft or hobby stores. Look at different types of leather products that you have at home. Shoe repair shops in your area hire leather workers that can tell you more about this craft.

Tell Me More:

Pedorthic Footwear Association
9861 Broken Land Pky., Suite 255
Columbia, MD 21046-1151

Shoe Service Institute of
  America Educational Library
5024-R Campbell Blvd.
Baltimore, MD 21236-5974

Upholsterers use common handtools.

Education and Training:

Most upholsterers train on-the-job or get basic training in high school, vocational school, or community college. Experienced upholsterers may become supervisors.

Job Outlook:

Poor

Average Earnings:

Low

What They Do: Upholsterers make new furniture and repair or replace old furniture. They use regular handtools like staple guns and pliers, and special tools like upholstery needles. When they recondition old furniture first they remove the old fabric, padding, and springs. When making new furniture they start with a wooden frame and add springs, padding, and cloth.

Working Conditions: Upholsterers usually work in ships or factories. They must be careful when using sharp tools and lifting heavy furniture. They stand and bend a lot when working.

Related Jobs: Furniture finisher, fur cutter, and pattern and model make

Subjects To Study Now and Later: English, mathematics, shop, and drafting

Getting Ready and Places to Go to Observe: Study the furniture in your home. Look for different types of fabric, look at the different way each piece is made. Find scraps of wood, fabric, and nails and upholster the wood on one side. Upholstery shops are listed in the telephone directory. Also, read the newspaper for ads that list this service.

Tell Me More:

Accrediting Commission of Career Schools and
    Colleges of Technology
2101 Wilson Blvd., Suite 302
Arlington, VA 22201

Dental Laboratory Technicians

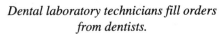

Dental laboratory technicians fill orders from dentists.

Education and Training:

It takes up to four years of on-the-job experience to be fully trained. There are also two-year vocational programs.

Job Outlook:

Good

Average Earnings:

Low - Medium

What They Do: Dental laboratory technicians follow dentists' orders to make dentures, crowns, and bridges. The dentist provides a mold of the patient's mouth to the technician. The technician uses plaster to make a model of the mouth. Using metal, porcelain, and very small tools, the technician uses the model to build and shape the dentist's order.

Working Conditions: Dental laboratory technicians work in clean, well-lighted areas. They work with different types of equipment, including Bunsen burners and hand tools.

Related Jobs: Orthotics technician, prosthetics technician, optician, and ophthalmic laboratory technician

Subjects To Study Now and Later: Biology, health, art, metal and wood shop, drafting, chemistry, mathematics, and English

Getting Ready and Places to Go to Observe: Ask your dentist and hygienist what they do to prepare a bridge or crown for a patient. What tools do they use to make a mold?

Tell Me More:

National Association of Dental
  Laboratories
555 E. Braddock Rd.
Alexandria, VA 22314

Commission on Dental Accreditation
American Dental Association
211 E. Chicago Ave.
Chicago, IL 60611
http://www.ada.org

Laborers

Laborers often learn on-the-job.

Education and Training:

Some companies require a high school diploma.

Job Outlook:

Good

Average Earnings:

Low

What They Do: Laborers usually work for construction or production companies. You can find laborers working in almost all types of trades or companies. Laborers perform many different jobs that help more skilled workers. The jobs may be moving boxes, cleaning machines, or supplying tools as needed. Some laborers do work which provides a service to people, such as car washing.

Working Conditions: Some laborers work outdoors and some work indoors. The work is often physical. Laborers may work nights and weekends.

Related Jobs: Handler, equipment cleaner, helper, machine operator, construction craft worker, assembler, mechanic, and repairer

Subjects To Study Now and Later: Mathematics, English, and shop

Getting Ready and Places to Go to Observe: Read about how different items work. These items can be cars, clocks, televisions, or just about anything. Also, read about how houses, bridges, and buildings are built. If you have a relative or neighbor who works for a construction or production company, ask them if you can go with them and watch people at work. Can you figure out who is the laborer and who is the skilled worker?

Tell Me More:

Laborers' International Union of North America
905 16th St. NW
Washington, DC 20006

Photographic Process Workers

Education and Training:

A high school diploma with some experience and knowledge about the field is preferred.

Job Outlook:

Poor

Average Earnings:

Low

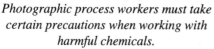
Photographic process workers must take certain precautions when working with harmful chemicals.

What They Do: Photographic process workers develop film, make prints and slides, and do related tasks requested by photographers. Some photographic process workers operate machinery that develops and makes prints from film very easily. Other photographic process workers make changes to film negatives by hand. Handwork is done very carefully.

Working Conditions: Photographic process workers work indoors in clean, photofinishing laboratories. Some use chemicals when developing and printing film.

Related Jobs: Chemical laboratory technician, crime laboratory technician, food tester, medical laboratory assistant, metallurgical technician, quality control technician, engraver, and photolithographer

Subjects To Study Now and Later: Art, photography, chemistry, and English

Getting Ready and Places to Go to Observe: Learning about photography is a fun hobby which will help you learn about the developing process. Some people set up a developing room in their homes. Many stores have automatic film developing equipment. If you have one near you, ask the manager if you can watch the worker operate it. Check with local colleges and schools near you to see if they have photography courses. The instructor might give you a tour of the laboratory.

Tell Me More:

Photo Marketing Association International
3000 Picture Place
Jackson, MI 49201

Transportation and Material Moving Occupations

Workers in these occupations operate the equipment used to move people and equipment. These are workers who drive vehicles on highways and streets, keep our trains running safely, and help move people and freight across land and water. People who work in this cluster may travel away from home often.

Busdrivers

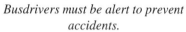

Busdrivers must be alert to prevent accidents.

 Education and Training:

Most companies prefer at least a high school education. State and Federal regulations must be met.

 Job Outlook:

Excellent

 Average Earnings:

Low

What They Do: Busdrivers drive and transport people in buses. They pick up children from homes and drive them to school. After school they take children back home. Busdrivers move people from one part of a town to another. People travel all over the country on buses. Busdrivers must be very good drivers because they are responsible for moving people safely and on time.

Working Conditions: Busdrivers sit for long periods of time. They drive in all types of weather. Nights, holidays, and weekend work may be required.

Related Jobs: Taxidriver, truckdriver, and chauffeur

Subjects To Study Now and Later: English, first aid, and auto mechanics

Getting Ready and Places to Go to Observe: Busdrivers should be in good health. Make eating well, exercising, and getting enough sleep a part of your lifestyle. Learn first-aid from a local Red Cross chapter. If you ride in a bus to school, watch what your busdriver is doing as the bus moves from one stop to another. Are you picked up and dropped off on time? Ride on a city bus to see different kinds of job duties.

 Tell Me More:

National School Transportation
   Association
P.O. Box 2639
Springfield, VA 22152

American Bus Association
1100 New York Ave. NW, Suite 1050
Washington, DC 20005

Rail Transportation Workers

Rail transportation workers make sure goods and passengers arrive safely and on time.

Education and Training:

A high school education is preferred. Training is often needed. Good hearing, eyesight, color vision and eye-hand coordination is necessary.

Job Outlook:

Poor

Average Earnings:

Medium

What They Do: Rail transportation workers move people and freight by trains, subways, and streetcars. There are many different types of rail transportation workers. Engineers are the workers who operate the trains. Other rail transportation workers are conductors who take care of freight and people traveling on trains. Subway operators guide subway trains and make sure people get on and off the subway safely. Streetcar operators collect fares from passengers and answer questions concerning schedules and routes.

Working Conditions: Some rail transportation workers spend most of the time outdoors. Others must travel for many days at a time if they work on a train as it moves from one train station to another. They often work evenings, weekends, and holidays.

Related Jobs: Freight conductor, conductor, signal operator, switch operator, brake operator, rail yard engineer, and locomotive engineer

Subjects To Study Now and Later: Social studies, auto mechanics, and English

Getting Ready and Places to Go to Observe: Read about the history of rail transportation. There are many good books about trains at the library. You may also find books about subways and streetcars. Visit a train station where you can watch rail transportation workers. Ride on a subway or streetcar if you have these in your community.

Tell Me More:

Association of American
    Railroads
50 F St. NW
Washington, DC 20001

Brotherhood of Locomotive
    Engineers
1370 Ontario Ave.
Cleveland, OH 44113-1702

Truckdrivers

Education and Training:

Many companies require at least a high school education. Federal and state regulations must also be met, which includes passing a variety of tests.

Job Outlook:

Good

Average Earnings:

Low - Medium

Truckdrivers spend most of the time behind the wheel.

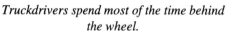

What They Do: Truckdrivers drive trucks to move freight from one place to another. Some truckdrivers, such as route drivers, travel within one city. Route drivers also have sales and customer service duties. A route driver often recommends products to a store manager and stocks the shelves. Others must travel long distances between cities. Truckdrivers inspect their trucks to make sure parts like brakes, windshield wipers, and lights are working.

Working Conditions: Truckdrivers must sit for long periods of time. Some must spend many days away from home. They also may have to do a lot of lifting.

Related Jobs: Ambulance driver, busdriver, chauffeur, and taxi driver

Subjects To Study Now and Later: Social studies, business, auto mechanics, and English

Getting Ready and Places to Go to Observe: Read about trucks and transportation. Moving freight is very important to the country's economy. Trucking is one of the major ways to move freight. It is easy to watch for big trucks when you are travelling on highways or streets. Visit your local market. Ask the manager if a route driver is making a delivery. Try to talk to the route driver to learn more about the job.

Tell Me More:

American Trucking Associations, Inc.
2200 Mill Road
Alexandria, VA 22314

American Trucking Association
Foundation
660 Roosevelt Ave.
Pawtucket, RI 02860

Youth
Jobs

There are many jobs that teach young people good skills, how to earn money and help prepare them for the world of work. These are a few examples. There are many more. Talk to your family about any jobs which are of interest to you.

Baby Sitters

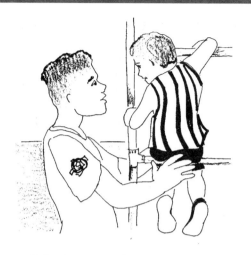

Education and Training:

Many baby sitters learn from helping care for brothers and sisters at home. Home economics classes and the ability to get along with others is important in this job. Look for babysitting classes in your community.

Job Outlook:

Excellent

Baby sitters must be responsible and prepared to act in an emergency.

What They Do: Baby sitters are hired to take care of one or more children, usually while parents are out of the house. They supervise, feed, dress, and bathe children as needed. Baby sitters often play games and toys with the children they are watching. Baby sitters are responsible for the safety and well-being of the children until the parents come home.

Working Conditions: Baby sitters work different hours depending on the job. Many baby sitters work nights and weekends. This job requires lifting.

Related Jobs: Fast food worker, camp counselor, home health aide, preschool worker, and private household worker

Subjects To Study Now and Later: Home economics, CPR (including infant CPR), first aid, early child development, English, and speech

Getting Ready and Places to Go to Observe: Learn more about baby sitting by helping care for younger brothers and sisters. Local recreation districts offer classes that teach about baby sitting. Ask parents of young children if you can talk to their baby sitter. Day care centers care for children outside the home. They can tell you more about baby sitting.

Tell Me More:

National Association for the Education
    of Young Children
1509 16th St. NW
Washington, DC 20036

Association for Childhood
    Education International
11501 Georgia Ave., Suite 315
Wheaton, MD 20902-1924

Bicycle Repairers

 Education and Training:

Most youth learn this job by keeping their own bicycles in good condition. There are many books on bicycle repair.

 Job Outlook:

Good

Bicycle repairers often learn from working on their own bikes.

What They Do: Bicycle repairers repair and service bicycles. First, they must find out what the problem is and then know how to repair the bicycle. They also clean bikes and do maintenance work to keep the bicycles in good condition.

Working Conditions: Bicycle repairers work indoors in repair shops and bike stores.

Related Jobs: Auto mechanic assistant, bicycle shop worker

Subjects To Study Now and Later: English, mathematics, and shop

Getting Ready and Places to Go to Observe: Visit a bicycle shop which does repairs. There are many bicycle magazines and books at the library to read. Keep your own and your family's bikes in good working condition. Some communities offer bicycle maintenance courses. Enroll in one if it's offered in your area.

 Tell Me More:

Look for bicycle magazines in your library. You'll find information about bikes and manufacturers.

Baggers

Baggers must be friendly and helpful to the store's customers.

Education and Training:

On-the-job training is often the way baggers learn this job. Experience working with the public is helpful.

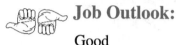

Job Outlook:

Good

What They Do: Baggers work in grocery stores, bagging groceries and assisting in other odd jobs. They help load groceries in the customer's car and bring carts back into the store. They need to bag the groceries in special ways that will not damage the goods.

Working Conditions: Baggers work inside grocery stores and outside when taking groceries to customer's cars. They usually work part-time, evenings and weekends. This job requires lifting.

Related Jobs: Cashier, food counter clerk, and retail clerk

Subjects To Study Now and Later: English, mathematics, and speech

Getting Ready and Places to Go to Observe: Local supermarkets hire baggers that you can watch at work. Notice the way that they bag the groceries. The heavy items are on the bottom of the bags and the items that can be crushed are on the top. Help your parents unload and put away the groceries when you get home.

Tell Me More:

National Retail Association
7th St. NW, Suite 1000
Washington, DC 20004
http://www.nrf.com

 Education and Training:

Training is usually required for this job. Many national youth associations offer training courses. Experience in working with people is helpful.

 Job Outlook:

Good

Camp counselors learn a lot while they work.

What They Do: Camp counselors plan, lead, and instruct campers in activities like swimming, hiking, and crafts. They also provide guidance and supervision for campers. Camp counselors usually work only during the summer break.

Working Conditions: Camp counselors usually work evenings and weekends. They sometimes work indoors, but most of their time is spent outdoors. Camp counselors must like working with people.

Related Jobs: Baby sitter, teacher, counselor, and recreation worker

Subjects To Study Now and Later: English, physical education, early child development, speech, and art

Getting Ready and Places to Go to Observe: Baby sitting is a good way to gain experience that will be helpful as a camp counselor. Local recreation departments sometimes offer classes in baby sitting. Good health is also important. Find out what camps are available in your area. Talk to teenagers that have experience as a camp counselor to find out more about this job.

 Tell Me More:

American Camping Association
5000 State Rd., 67 North
Martinsville, IN 46151

National Recreation and Park
  Association
Division of Professional Services
2775 South Quincy St., Suite 300
Arlington, VA 22206
http://www.nrpa.org

Fast Food Workers

Fast food workers are in great demand.

 Education and Training:

Training on-the-job is usually the way that fast food workers learn this job.

 Job Outlook:

Excellent

What They Do: Fast food workers take orders for food and beverages. They collect money and serve customers. Other duties include stocking supplies and cleanup. Some help cook and prepare the food. Fast food workers must be clean, be courteous to customers, and be willing to be hard working.

Working Conditions: Fast food workers usually work some evenings and weekends. They must be friendly and like working with people. Fast food workers usually wear uniforms.

Related Jobs: Food service worker, flight attendant, bellhop, and kitchen helper

Subjects To Study Now and Later: English, mathematics, speech, and home economics

Getting Ready and Places to Go to Observe: Helping out in the kitchen at home is a good way to get experience needed for this job. Ask if students can volunteer to help in your school cafeteria. There are many different types of fast food restaurants nearby that you can visit to learn more about this job.

 Tell Me More:

The National Restaurant
   Association
1200 17th St. NW
Washington, DC 20036-3097

The Educational Foundation of the
   National Restaurant Association
250 South Wacker Dr., Suite 1400
Chicago, IL 60606

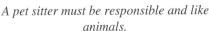

A pet sitter must be responsible and like animals.

Education and Training:

Most pet sitters learn on-the-job. The pet owners teach the pet sitter about the special needs of the animals.

Job Outlook:

Good

What They Do: Pet sitters take care of animals when their owners are away. They make sure there is plenty of food and water. Some animals need to be walked or taken outside each day. Other animals, like fish, need to be checked each day to be sure their environment is safe and healthy.

Working Conditions: Pet sitters' work is off and on depending on vacation schedules. This job usually takes a small amount of time each day for as many days as the owner is away.

Related Jobs: Baby sitter, yard worker, camp counselor, and animal care taker

Subjects To Study Now and Later: English, mathematics, speech, and science

Getting Ready and Places to Go to Observe: Taking care of your own pet is a good way to learn about the special needs of animals. Check out your local library to read about pet care. Learn about other kinds of animals and the different type of care that they need. Visit your local animal shelter or zoo to see people taking care of many types of animals. Veterinarians can give you more information about pet care.

Tell Me More:

The Humane Society of the U.S.
2100 L St. NW
Washington, DC 20037-1598

National Animal Control
  Association
P.O. Box 480851
Kansas City, MO 64148-0851

Referees and Umpires

 Education and Training:

Referees and umpires attend special training programs. These programs are usually through the local sport leagues, a city recreation department, or a local high school. A knowledge of sports is helpful.

 Job Outlook:

Good

Referees and umpires make quick calls about the game.

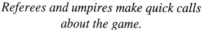

What They Do: Referees and umpires are officials that enforce set rules in sports. They often work at team sporting events. Umpires work at baseball games and referees work at games like basketball, soccer, and football. They wear special uniforms and use hand signals and whistles to indicate their decision.

Working Conditions: Referees and umpires work inside or outside depending on the type of sport. They often work evenings and weekends.

Related Jobs: Physical education teacher, recreational worker, and camp counselor

Subjects To Study Now and Later: Physical education, English, mathematics, and speech

Getting Ready and Places to Go to Observe: Become involved in team sports in your area. Playing sports is a good way to learn the rules and watch referees and umpires at work. Many recreation departments have youth programs that train teenagers to umpire or referee games for younger teams. Attend games in your hometown or watch professional sports on television to see referees and umpires at work.

 Tell Me More:

American Alliance for Health, Physical Education, and Recreation
1900 Association Drive
Reston, VA 22091

Yard Workers

Yard workers are needed mostly in the spring and summer.

Education and Training:

Most yard workers learn this job at home helping out with family yard work.

Job Outlook:

Good

What They Do: Yard workers have many jobs that they perform. They mow lawns, use a weedeater to cut tall grass, and weed flowerbeds. They may help with special landscape projects that require removing brush, moving rocks, and hauling dirt.

Working Conditions: Yard workers work outdoors in all types of weather. This job requires bending and lifting. Knowing how to use equipment like lawn mowers and weedeaters is necessary.

Related Jobs: Gardener, nursery worker, and tree trimmer

Subjects To Study Now and Later: Horticulture, English, mathematics, and shop

Getting Ready and Places to Go to Observe: Helping your family with yard work is a good way to learn how to care for grass and plants. Grow your own small garden and care for it. Learn the names of plants and trees in your yard. A visit to the nursery can teach you more about plants and trees. Take a walk in your yard or a park and talk about the different types of plants and trees. Watch for changes with each new season.

Tell Me More:

American Society of Landscape
    Architects
Career Information
4401 Connecticut Ave. NW
Washington, DC 20008

Council of Landscape
Architectural Reg. Boards
12700 Fair Lakes Circle, Suite 110
Fairfax, VA 22033
Email: *clarb2@aol.com*

Index